VB.NET AND
OLEDB

Working with the Dataset

Richard Thomas Edwards

CONTENTS

Welcome To OLEDB 3

The OLEDB Objects 5

    Connection, Command and DataAdapter 5

    Connection and DataAdapter...6

    Command and DataAdapter...6

    DataAdapter..6

    Connection, Command and DataReader 6

    Command and Reader..7

Working with the Dataset..8

    Doing it Manually 9

ASP Examples 11

ASPX Examples 21

HTA Examples 30

HTML Examples...40

Excel Examples...49

Delimited Text Examples 58

XML Examples 75

XSL Examples 89

    Single Line Horizontal..89

    Multi Line Horizontal 91

Single Line Vertical 94

Multi Line Vertical 96

Single Line Horizontal 98

Multi Line Horizontal 100

Single Line Vertical 102

Multi Line Vertical 104

Stylesheets 107

Welcome To OLEDB
What is OLEDB

THE FIRST THING HAT SHOULD POP OUT AT YOU IS THE FACT THAT THIS ENTIRE BOOK IS DEDICATED TO THE USE OF THE DATASET. The others will be covered in separate books. Now, it is time to explore OLEDB. So, what is OLEDB and why is it separated from ODBC or SQL Client?

OLEDB stands for Object Linking and Embedding Database. It has been around since 1996. In fact, there was an OLE control shipped with VB4, VB5 and VB6.

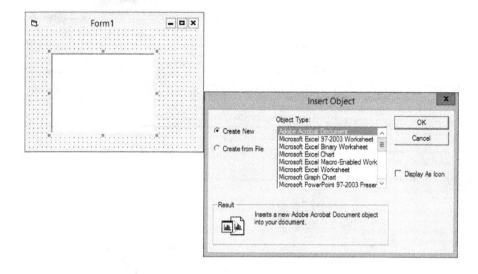

Above is an image of what happened when the control was painted onto a VB6.

Notice that the control prompts you to add an embedded object into the control and once you do, because the control can be bound to a database that accepts very large files -blobs- you can save the imbedded information.

The OLEDB Objects
Connection, Command DataReader and
DataAdapter

I F YOU HAVE BEEN WORKING WITH .NET FOR SOME TIME AND HAVE BEEN WORKING WITH OLEDB, ODBC, OR SQL CLIENT, YOU KNOW THEY ALL LOOK PRETTY MUCH THE SAME. You have the connection; the command; and you populate the information using a DataReader or A DataAdapter. Below, is pretty much how all of it works together:

```
Dim cnstr As String – ""
Dim strQuery As String = ""
Connection, Command and DataAdapter


Dim cn as new System.Data.OLEDB.OLEDBConnection()
Cn.ConnectionString = cnstr
Cn.Open()


Dim cmd as new System.Data.OLEDB.OLEDBCommand()
Cmd.Connection = cn
Cmd.CommandType = CommandTypeText
Cmd.ExecuteNonQuery()


Dim DA as System.Data.OLEDB.OLEDBDataAdatper(cmd)
```

Connection and DataAdapter

```
Dim cn as new System.Data.OLEDB.OLEDBConnection()
Cn.ConnectionString = cnstr
Cn.Open()

Dim DA as System.Data.OLEDB.OLEDBDataAdatper(strQuery, cn)
```

Command and DataAdapter

```
Dim cmd as new System.Data.OLEDB.OLEDBCommand()
Cmd.Connection =  new System.Data.OLEDB.OLEDBConnection
Cmd.Connection.ConnectionString = cnstr
Cmd.Connection.Open()
Cmd.CommandType = CommandTypeText
Cmd.ExecuteNonQuery()

Dim DA as System.Data.OLEDB.OLEDBDataAdatper(cmd)
```

DataAdapter

```
Dim DA as System.Data.OLEDB.OLEDBDataAdatper(strQuery, cnstr)
```

Connection, Command and DataReader

```
Dim cn as new System.Data.OLEDB.OLEDBConnection()
Cn.ConnectionString = cnstr
Cn.Open()

Dim cmd as new System.Data.OLEDB.OLEDBCommand()
Cmd.Connection = cn
```

```
Cmd.CommandType = CommandTypeText
Dim dr As System.Data.OLEDB.OLEDBDataReader = cmd.ExecuteReader()
```

Command and Reader

```
Dim cmd as new System.Data.OLEDB.OLEDBCommand()
Cmd.Connection = new System.Data.OLEDB.OLEDBConnection
Cmd.Connection.ConnectionString = cnstr
Cmd.Connection.Open()
Cmd.CommandType = CommandTypeText
Dim dr As System.Data.OLEDB.OLEDBDataReader = cmd.ExecuteReader()
```

Working with the Dataset

Bound or unbound

THIS MAY COME A SURPRISE TO YOU BUT THE DATASET CAN BE POPULATED AS A BOUND OBJECT OR AN UNBOUND OBJECT. Let's start with the normal way first and then I'll show you how it can be used in the unbound mode.

Okay, so you have an OLEDBDataAdapter filled with the information you want to bind to the System.Data.Dataset.

```
Dim ds as new System.Data.Dataset
DA.Fill(ds)
You can also specify the tablename here, too.
DA.Fill(ds, "Products")
```

Now, you have a Dataset that is populated with one Table. If you added a DataGridView to the from and this code is running in the form, you simply do the following:

```
DataGridView1.DataSource = ds.Tables(0)
```

That will populate the DataGridView. Notice that you don't just type in the DataSource as ds. If you did do that: DataGridView1.DataSource = ds, when run, the DataGridView1 will be empty.

Doing it Manually

```vb
Dim ds As New System.Data.DataSet()
        Dim dt As New System.Data.DataTable()
        ds.Tables.Add(dt)

        Dim svc As Object = GetObject("winmgmts:\\.\Root\CIMV2")
        Dim objs = svc.InstancesOf("Win32_Process")
        For Each obj In objs
            For Each prop As Object In obj.Properties_
                ds.Tables(0).Columns.Add(prop.Name,
GetType(System.String))
            Next
            Exit For
        Next

        Dim x As Integer = 0
        Dim y As Integer = 0

        For Each obj In objs
            ds.Tables(0).Rows.Add()
            For Each prop As Object In obj.Properties_
                ds.Tables(0).Rows(y).Item(prop.Name) =
GetValue(prop.Name, obj)
            Next
            y = y + 1
        Next

        DataGridView1.DataSource = ds.Tables(0)



    Public Function GetValue(ByVal name As String, ByVal obj As
Object) As String
```

```vb
        Dim pos As Integer = InStr(obj.GetObjectText_, vbTab &
name & " = ")

        If pos Then

            Dim tempstr As String = Mid(obj.GetObjectText_, pos +
Len(name & " = "), Len(obj.GetObjectText_))
            pos = InStr(tempstr, ";")
            tempstr = Mid$(tempstr, 1, pos - 1)
            tempstr = Replace(tempstr, Chr(34), "")
            tempstr = Replace(tempstr, "{", "")
            tempstr = Replace(tempstr, "}", "")
            If tempstr.Length > 14 Then
                If obj.Properties_.Item(name).CIMType = 101 Then
                    tempstr = Mid(tempstr, 5, 2) & "/" & _
                              Mid(tempstr, 7, 2) & "/" & _
                              Mid(tempstr, 1, 4) & " " & _
                              Mid(tempstr, 9, 2) & ":" & _
                              Mid(tempstr, 11, 2) & ":" & _
                              Mid(tempstr, 13, 2)
                End If
            End If
            GetValue = tempstr
        Else
            GetValue = ""
        End If

    End Function
```

ASP Examples

B ELOW ARE EXAMPLES OF OLEDB USING A DATASET.

Reports

Horizontal

```
Dim cnstr as String = "Provider=Microsoft.Jet.OLEDB.4.0;Data
Source="C:\Program Files (x86)\Microsoft Visual
Studio\VB98\NWIND.MDB""
Dim strQuery as String = "Select * From [Products]"

Dim cn As System.Data.OleDb.OleDbConnection = new
System.Data.OleDb.OleDbConnection(cnstr)
cn.Open()

Dim cmd As System.Data.OleDb.OleDbCommand = new
System.Data.OleDb.OleDbCommand()
cmd.Connection = cn
cmd.CommandType = 1
cmd.CommandText = strQuery
cmd.ExecuteNonquery()
```

```
Dim da As System.Data.OleDb.OleDbDataAdapter = new
System.Data.OleDb.OleDbDataAdapter(cmd)

Dim ds as new System.Data.DataSet
da.Fill(ds, "Products")

Dim ws As Object = CreateObject("WScript.Shell")
Dim fso As Object = CreateObject("Scripting.FileSystemObject")
Dim txtstream as Object = fso.OpenTextFile(ws.CurrentDirectory +
"\Products.asp", 2, True, -2)
txtstream.WriteLine("<hmtl>")
txtstream.WriteLine("<head>")
txtstream.WriteLine("<title>Products</title>")
txtstream.WriteLine("<style type='text/css'>")
txtstream.WriteLine("th")
txtstream.WriteLine(" {")
txtstream.WriteLine("    COLOR: darkred;")
txtstream.WriteLine("    BACKGROUND-COLOR: #eeeeee;")
txtstream.WriteLine("    FONT-FAMILY:font-family: Cambria, serif;")
txtstream.WriteLine("    FONT-SIZE: 12px;")
txtstream.WriteLine("    text-align: left;")
txtstream.WriteLine("    white-Space: nowrap='nowrap';")
txtstream.WriteLine("}")
txtstream.WriteLine("td")
txtstream.WriteLine(" {")
txtstream.WriteLine("    COLOR: navy;")
txtstream.WriteLine("    BACKGROUND-COLOR: #eeeeee;")
txtstream.WriteLine("    FONT-FAMILY: font-family: Cambria, serif;")
txtstream.WriteLine("    FONT-SIZE: 12px;")
txtstream.WriteLine("    text-align: left;")
txtstream.WriteLine("    white-Space: nowrap='nowrap';")
txtstream.WriteLine("}")
txtstream.WriteLine("</style>")

txtstream.WriteLine("</head>")
txtstream.WriteLine("<body>")
txtstream.WriteLine("<center>")
```

```vb
txtstream.WriteLine("</br>")
txtstream.WriteLine("<table border=0 cellspacing=3 cellpadding=3>")
txtstream.WriteLine("<%")
txtstream.WriteLine("Response.Write(""<tr>"" & vbcrlf)")
For Each col as System.Data.DataColumn in ds.Tables(0).Columns
txtstream.WriteLine("Response.Write(""<th align='left'
nowrap='nowrap'>" & col.Caption & "</th>"" & vbcrlf)")
Next
txtstream.WriteLine("Response.Write(""</tr>"" & vbcrlf)")

for each row as System.Data.DataRow in ds.Tables(0).Rows
txtstream.WriteLine("Response.Write(""<tr>"" & vbcrlf)")
For Each col as System.Data.DataColumn in ds.Tables(0).Columns
txtstream.WriteLine("Response.Write(""<td  align='left'
nowrap='nowrap'>" & row.Item(col.Caption) & "</td>"" & vbcrlf)")
Next

txtstream.WriteLine("Response.Write(""</tr>"" & vbcrlf)")

Next
txtstream.WriteLine("%>")
txtstream.WriteLine("</table>")
txtstream.WriteLine("</body>")
txtstream.WriteLine("</html>")
txtstream.Close()


     Vertical


Dim cnstr as String = "Provider=Microsoft.Jet.OLEDB.4.0;Data
Source=""C:\Program Files (x86)\Microsoft Visual
Studio\VB98\NWIND.MDB"""
Dim strQuery as String = "Select * From [Products]"

Dim cn As System.Data.OleDb.OleDbConnection  = new
System.Data.OleDb.OleDbConnection(cnstr)
```

```
cn.Open()

Dim cmd As System.Data.OleDb.OleDbCommand = new
System.Data.OleDb.OleDbCommand()
cmd.Connection = cn
cmd.CommandType = 1
cmd.CommandText = strQuery
cmd.ExecuteNonquery()

Dim da As System.Data.OleDb.OleDbDataAdapter = new
System.Data.OleDb.OleDbDataAdapter(cmd)

Dim ds as new System.Data.DataSet
da.Fill(ds, "Products")

Dim ws As Object = CreateObject("WScript.Shell")
Dim fso As Object = CreateObject("Scripting.FileSystemObject")
Dim txtstream as Object = fso.OpenTextFile(ws.CurrentDirectory +
"\Products.asp", 2, True, -2)
txtstream.WriteLine("<hmtl>")
txtstream.WriteLine("<head>")
txtstream.WriteLine("<title>Products</title>")
txtstream.WriteLine("<style type='text/css'>")
txtstream.WriteLine("th")
txtstream.WriteLine(" {")
txtstream.WriteLine("   COLOR: darkred;")
txtstream.WriteLine("   BACKGROUND-COLOR: #eeeeee;")
txtstream.WriteLine("   FONT-FAMILY:font-family: Cambria, serif;")
txtstream.WriteLine("   FONT-SIZE: 12px;")
txtstream.WriteLine("   text-align: left;")
txtstream.WriteLine("   white-Space: nowrap='nowrap';")
txtstream.WriteLine("}")
txtstream.WriteLine("td")
txtstream.WriteLine(" {")
txtstream.WriteLine("   COLOR: navy;")
txtstream.WriteLine("   BACKGROUND-COLOR: #eeeeee;")
txtstream.WriteLine("   FONT-FAMILY: font-family: Cambria, serif;")
```

```
txtstream.WriteLine("    FONT-SIZE: 12px;")
txtstream.WriteLine("    text-align: left;")
txtstream.WriteLine("    white-Space: nowrap='nowrap';")
txtstream.WriteLine("}")
txtstream.WriteLine("</style>")

txtstream.WriteLine("</head>")
txtstream.WriteLine("<body>")
txtstream.WriteLine("<center>")
txtstream.WriteLine("</br>")
txtstream.WriteLine("<table border=0 cellspacing=3 cellpadding=3>")
txtstream.WriteLine("<%")
For Each col as System.Data.DataColumn in ds.Tables(0).Columns
txtstream.WriteLine("Response.Write(""<tr><th align='left'
nowrap='nowrap'>" & col.Caption & "</th>""" & vbcrlf)")
for each row as System.Data.DataRow in ds.Tables(0).Rows
txtstream.WriteLine("Response.Write(""<td  align='left'
nowrap='true'><input type=text value=""" & row.Item(col.Caption) &
"""></input></td>""" & vbcrlf)")

Next
txtstream.WriteLine("Response.Write(""</tr>""" & vbcrlf)")
Next
txtstream.WriteLine("%>")
txtstream.WriteLine("</table>")
txtstream.WriteLine("</body>")
txtstream.WriteLine("</html>")
txtstream.Close()
```

Tables

Horizontal

```vb
Dim cnstr as String = "Provider=Microsoft.Jet.OLEDB.4.0;Data
Source="C:\Program Files (x86)\Microsoft Visual
Studio\VB98\NWIND.MDB""
Dim strQuery as String = "Select * From [Products]"

Dim cn As System.Data.OleDb.OleDbConnection = new
System.Data.OleDb.OleDbConnection(cnstr)
cn.Open()

Dim cmd As System.Data.OleDb.OleDbCommand = new
System.Data.OleDb.OleDbCommand()
cmd.Connection = cn
cmd.CommandType = 1
cmd.CommandText = strQuery
cmd.ExecuteNonquery()

Dim da As System.Data.OleDb.OleDbDataAdapter = new
System.Data.OleDb.OleDbDataAdapter(cmd)

Dim ds as new System.Data.DataSet
da.Fill(ds, "Products")

Dim ws As Object = CreateObject("WScript.Shell")
Dim fso As Object = CreateObject("Scripting.FileSystemObject")
Dim txtstream as Object = fso.OpenTextFile(ws.CurrentDirectory +
"\Products.asp", 2, True, -2)
txtstream.WriteLine("<hmtl>")
txtstream.WriteLine("<head>")
txtstream.WriteLine("<title>Products</title>")
txtstream.WriteLine("<style type='text/css'>")
txtstream.WriteLine("th")
txtstream.WriteLine(" {")
txtstream.WriteLine("    COLOR: darkred;")
txtstream.WriteLine("    BACKGROUND-COLOR: #eeeeee;")
txtstream.WriteLine("    FONT-FAMILY:font-family: Cambria, serif;")
```

```vbnet
txtstream.WriteLine("    FONT-SIZE: 12px;")
txtstream.WriteLine("    text-align: left;")
txtstream.WriteLine("    white-Space: nowrap='nowrap';")
txtstream.WriteLine("}")
txtstream.WriteLine("td")
txtstream.WriteLine(" {")
txtstream.WriteLine("    COLOR: navy;")
txtstream.WriteLine("    BACKGROUND-COLOR: #eeeeee;")
txtstream.WriteLine("    FONT-FAMILY: font-family: Cambria, serif;")
txtstream.WriteLine("    FONT-SIZE: 12px;")
txtstream.WriteLine("    text-align: left;")
txtstream.WriteLine("    white-Space: nowrap='nowrap';")
txtstream.WriteLine("}")
txtstream.WriteLine("</style>")

txtstream.WriteLine("</head>")
txtstream.WriteLine("<body>")
txtstream.WriteLine("<center>")
txtstream.WriteLine("</br>")
txtstream.WriteLine("<table style='border:Double;border-width:1px;border-color:navy;' rules=all frames=both cellpadding=2 cellspacing=2 Width=0>")
txtstream.WriteLine("<%")
txtstream.WriteLine("Response.Write(""<tr>"" & vbcrlf)")
For Each col as System.Data.DataColumn in ds.Tables(0).Columns
txtstream.WriteLine("Response.Write(""<th align='left' nowrap='nowrap'>" & col.Caption & "</th>"" & vbcrlf)")
Next
txtstream.WriteLine("Response.Write(""</tr>"" & vbcrlf)")

for each row as System.Data.DataRow in ds.Tables(0).Rows
txtstream.WriteLine("Response.Write(""<tr>"" & vbcrlf)")
For Each col as System.Data.DataColumn in ds.Tables(0).Columns
txtstream.WriteLine("Response.Write(""<td align='left' nowrap='nowrap'>" & row.Item(col.Caption) & "</td>"" & vbcrlf)")
Next
```

```
txtstream.WriteLine("Response.Write(""</tr>"" & vbcrlf)")

Next
txtstream.WriteLine("%>")
txtstream.WriteLine("</table>")
txtstream.WriteLine("</body>")
txtstream.WriteLine("</html>")
txtstream.Close()
```

Vertical

```
Dim cnstr as String = "Provider=Microsoft.Jet.OLEDB.4.0;Data
Source="C:\Program Files (x86)\Microsoft Visual
Studio\VB98\NWIND.MDB""
Dim strQuery as String = "Select * From [Products]"

Dim cn As System.Data.OleDb.OleDbConnection  = new
System.Data.OleDb.OleDbConnection(cnstr)
cn.Open()

Dim cmd As System.Data.OleDb.OleDbCommand  = new
System.Data.OleDb.OleDbCommand()
cmd.Connection = cn
cmd.CommandType = 1
cmd.CommandText = strQuery
cmd.ExecuteNonquery()

Dim da As System.Data.OleDb.OleDbDataAdapter  = new
System.Data.OleDb.OleDbDataAdapter(cmd)

Dim ds as new System.Data.DataSet
da.Fill(ds, "Products")
```

```
Dim ws As Object = CreateObject("WScript.Shell")
Dim fso As Object = CreateObject("Scripting.FileSystemObject")
Dim txtstream as Object = fso.OpenTextFile(ws.CurrentDirectory +
"\Products.asp", 2, True, -2)
txtstream.WriteLine("<hmtl>")
txtstream.WriteLine("<head>")
txtstream.WriteLine("<title>Products</title>")
txtstream.WriteLine("<style type='text/css'>")
txtstream.WriteLine("th")
txtstream.WriteLine(" {")
txtstream.WriteLine("    COLOR: darkred;")
txtstream.WriteLine("    BACKGROUND-COLOR: #eeeeee;")
txtstream.WriteLine("    FONT-FAMILY:font-family: Cambria, serif;")
txtstream.WriteLine("    FONT-SIZE: 12px;")
txtstream.WriteLine("    text-align: left;")
txtstream.WriteLine("    white-Space: nowrap='nowrap';")
txtstream.WriteLine("}")
txtstream.WriteLine("td")
txtstream.WriteLine(" {")
txtstream.WriteLine("    COLOR: navy;")
txtstream.WriteLine("    BACKGROUND-COLOR: #eeeeee;")
txtstream.WriteLine("    FONT-FAMILY: font-family: Cambria, serif;")
txtstream.WriteLine("    FONT-SIZE: 12px;")
txtstream.WriteLine("    text-align: left;")
txtstream.WriteLine("    white-Space: nowrap='nowrap';")
txtstream.WriteLine("}")
txtstream.WriteLine("</style>")

txtstream.WriteLine("</head>")
txtstream.WriteLine("<body>")
txtstream.WriteLine("<center>")
txtstream.WriteLine("</br>")
txtstream.WriteLine("</br>")
txtstream.WriteLine("<table style='border:Double;border-
width:1px;border-color:navy;' rules=all frames=both cellpadding=2
cellspacing=2 Width=0>")
```

```vb
txtstream.WriteLine("<%")
txtstream.WriteLine("Response.Write(""<tr>"" & vbcrlf)")
For Each col as System.Data.DataColumn in ds.Tables(0).Columns
txtstream.WriteLine("Response.Write(""<th align='left'
nowrap='nowrap'>" & col.Caption & "</th>"" & vbcrlf)")
Next
txtstream.WriteLine("Response.Write(""</tr>"" & vbcrlf)")

for each row as System.Data.DataRow in ds.Tables(0).Rows
txtstream.WriteLine("Response.Write(""<tr>"" & vbcrlf)")
For Each col as System.Data.DataColumn in ds.Tables(0).Columns
txtstream.WriteLine("Response.Write(""<td  align='left'
nowrap='nowrap'>" & row.Item(col.Caption) & "</td>"" & vbcrlf)")
Next

txtstream.WriteLine("Response.Write(""</tr>"" & vbcrlf)")

Next
txtstream.WriteLine("%>")
txtstream.WriteLine("</table>")
txtstream.WriteLine("</body>")
txtstream.WriteLine("</html>")
txtstream.Close()
```

ASPX Examples

B ELOW ARE EXAMPLES OF OLEDB USING A DATASET.

Reports

Horizontal

```
Dim cnstr as String = "Provider=Microsoft.Jet.OLEDB.4.0;Data
Source=C:\NWIND.MDB"
Dim strQuery as String = "Select * From [Products]"

Dim cn As System.Data.OleDb.OleDbConnection  = new
System.Data.OleDb.OleDbConnection(cnstr)
cn.Open()

Dim cmd As System.Data.OleDb.OleDbCommand  = new
System.Data.OleDb.OleDbCommand()
cmd.Connection = cn
cmd.CommandType = 1
cmd.CommandText = strQuery
cmd.ExecuteNonquery()
```

```
Dim da As System.Data.OleDb.OleDbDataAdapter = new
System.Data.OleDb.OleDbDataAdapter(cmd)

Dim ds as new System.Data.DataSet
da.Fill(ds, "Products")

Dim ws As Object = CreateObject("WScript.Shell")
Dim fso As Object = CreateObject("Scripting.FileSystemObject")
Dim txtstream as Object = fso.OpenTextFile(ws.CurrentDirectory +
"\Products.aspx", 2, True, -2)
txtstream.WriteLine("<hmtl>")
txtstream.WriteLine("<head>")
txtstream.WriteLine("<title>Products</title>")
txtstream.WriteLine("<style type='text/css'>")
txtstream.WriteLine("th")
txtstream.WriteLine("{")
txtstream.WriteLine("    COLOR: darkred;")
txtstream.WriteLine("    BACKGROUND-COLOR: #eeeeee;")
txtstream.WriteLine("    FONT-FAMILY:font-family: Cambria, serif;")
txtstream.WriteLine("    FONT-SIZE: 12px;")
txtstream.WriteLine("    text-align: left;")
txtstream.WriteLine("    white-Space: nowrap='nowrap';")
txtstream.WriteLine("}")
txtstream.WriteLine("td")
txtstream.WriteLine("{")
txtstream.WriteLine("    COLOR: navy;")
txtstream.WriteLine("    BACKGROUND-COLOR: #eeeeee;")
txtstream.WriteLine("    FONT-FAMILY: font-family: Cambria, serif;")
txtstream.WriteLine("    FONT-SIZE: 12px;")
txtstream.WriteLine("    text-align: left;")
txtstream.WriteLine("    white-Space: nowrap='nowrap';")
txtstream.WriteLine("}")
txtstream.WriteLine("</style>")
txtstream.WriteLine("</head>")
txtstream.WriteLine("<body>")
txtstream.WriteLine("<center>")
txtstream.WriteLine("</br>")
```

```
txtstream.WriteLine("<table border=0 cellspacing=3 cellpadding=3>")
txtstream.WriteLine("Response.Write(""<tr>"" & vbcrlf)")
For Each col as System.Data.DataColumn in ds.Tables(0).Columns
txtstream.WriteLine("Response.Write(""<th align='left'
nowrap='nowrap'>" & col.Caption & "</th>"" & vbcrlf)")
Next
txtstream.WriteLine("Response.Write(""</tr>"" & vbcrlf)")

for each row as System.Data.DataRow in ds.Tables(0).Rows
txtstream.WriteLine("Response.Write(""<tr>"" & vbcrlf)")
For Each col as System.Data.DataColumn in ds.Tables(0).Columns
txtstream.WriteLine("Response.Write(""<td  align='left'
nowrap='nowrap'>" & row.Item(col.Caption) & "</td>"" & vbcrlf)")
Next

txtstream.WriteLine("Response.Write(""</tr>"" & vbcrlf)")

Next
txtstream.WriteLine("%>")
txtstream.WriteLine("</table>")
txtstream.WriteLine("</body>")
txtstream.WriteLine("</html>")
txtstream.Close()
```

Vertical

```
Dim cnstr as String = "Provider=Microsoft.Jet.OLEDB.4.0;Data
Source=C:\NWIND.MDB"
Dim strQuery as String = "Select * From [Products]"

Dim cn As System.Data.OleDb.OleDbConnection  = new
System.Data.OleDb.OleDbConnection(cnstr)
cn.Open()
```

```
Dim cmd As System.Data.OleDb.OleDbCommand = new
System.Data.OleDb.OleDbCommand()
cmd.Connection = cn
cmd.CommandType = 1
cmd.CommandText = strQuery
cmd.ExecuteNonquery()

Dim da As System.Data.OleDb.OleDbDataAdapter = new
System.Data.OleDb.OleDbDataAdapter(cmd)

Dim ds as new System.Data.DataSet
da.Fill(ds, "Products")

Dim ws As Object = CreateObject("WScript.Shell")
Dim fso As Object = CreateObject("Scripting.FileSystemObject")
Dim txtstream as Object = fso.OpenTextFile(ws.CurrentDirectory +
"\Products.aspx", 2, True, -2)
txtstream.WriteLine("<hmtl>")
txtstream.WriteLine("<head>")
txtstream.WriteLine("<title>Products</title>")
txtstream.WriteLine("<style type='text/css'>")
txtstream.WriteLine("th")
txtstream.WriteLine("{")
txtstream.WriteLine("    COLOR: darkred;")
txtstream.WriteLine("    BACKGROUND-COLOR: #eeeeee;")
txtstream.WriteLine("    FONT-FAMILY:font-family: Cambria, serif;")
txtstream.WriteLine("    FONT-SIZE: 12px;")
txtstream.WriteLine("    text-align: left;")
txtstream.WriteLine("    white-Space: nowrap='nowrap';")
txtstream.WriteLine("}")
txtstream.WriteLine("td")
txtstream.WriteLine("{")
txtstream.WriteLine("    COLOR: navy;")
txtstream.WriteLine("    BACKGROUND-COLOR: #eeeeee;")
txtstream.WriteLine("    FONT-FAMILY: font-family: Cambria, serif;")
txtstream.WriteLine("    FONT-SIZE: 12px;")
txtstream.WriteLine("    text-align: left;")
```

```
txtstream.WriteLine("    white-Space: nowrap='nowrap';")
txtstream.WriteLine("}")
txtstream.WriteLine("</style>")
txtstream.WriteLine("</head>")
txtstream.WriteLine("<body>")
txtstream.WriteLine("<center>")
txtstream.WriteLine("</br>")
txtstream.WriteLine("<table border=0 cellspacing=3 cellpadding=3>")
For Each col as System.Data.DataColumn in ds.Tables(0).Columns
txtstream.WriteLine("Response.Write(""<tr><th align='left'
nowrap='nowrap'>" & col.Caption & "</th>"" & vbcrlf)")
for each row as System.Data.DataRow in ds.Tables(0).Rows
txtstream.WriteLine("Response.Write(""<td  align='left'
nowrap='true'><input type=text value=""" & row.Item(col.Caption) &
"""></input></td>"" & vbcrlf)")

Next
txtstream.WriteLine("Response.Write(""</tr>"" & vbcrlf)")
Next
txtstream.WriteLine("%>")
txtstream.WriteLine("</table>")
txtstream.WriteLine("</body>")
txtstream.WriteLine("</html>")
txtstream.Close()
```

Tables

Horizontal

```
Dim cnstr as String = "Provider=Microsoft.Jet.OLEDB.4.0;Data
Source=C:\NWIND.MDB"
Dim strQuery as String = "Select * From [Products]"

Dim cn As System.Data.OleDb.OleDbConnection  = new
System.Data.OleDb.OleDbConnection(cnstr)
cn.Open()
```

```
Dim cmd As System.Data.OleDb.OleDbCommand = new
System.Data.OleDb.OleDbCommand()
cmd.Connection = cn
cmd.CommandType = 1
cmd.CommandText = strQuery
cmd.ExecuteNonquery()

Dim da As System.Data.OleDb.OleDbDataAdapter = new
System.Data.OleDb.OleDbDataAdapter(cmd)

Dim ds as new System.Data.DataSet
da.Fill(ds, "Products")

Dim ws As Object = CreateObject("WScript.Shell")
Dim fso As Object = CreateObject("Scripting.FileSystemObject")
Dim txtstream as Object = fso.OpenTextFile(ws.CurrentDirectory +
"\Products.aspx", 2, True, -2)
txtstream.WriteLine("<hmtl>")
txtstream.WriteLine("<head>")
txtstream.WriteLine("<title>Products</title>")
txtstream.WriteLine("<style type='text/css'>")
txtstream.WriteLine("th")
txtstream.WriteLine("{")
txtstream.WriteLine("    COLOR: darkred;")
txtstream.WriteLine("    BACKGROUND-COLOR: #eeeeee;")
txtstream.WriteLine("    FONT-FAMILY:font-family: Cambria, serif;")
txtstream.WriteLine("    FONT-SIZE: 12px;")
txtstream.WriteLine("    text-align: left;")
txtstream.WriteLine("    white-Space: nowrap='nowrap';")
txtstream.WriteLine("}")
txtstream.WriteLine("td")
txtstream.WriteLine("{")
txtstream.WriteLine("    COLOR: navy;")
txtstream.WriteLine("    BACKGROUND-COLOR: #eeeeee;")
txtstream.WriteLine("    FONT-FAMILY: font-family: Cambria, serif;")
txtstream.WriteLine("    FONT-SIZE: 12px;")
txtstream.WriteLine("    text-align: left;")
```

```
txtstream.WriteLine("    white-Space: nowrap='nowrap';")
txtstream.WriteLine("}")
txtstream.WriteLine("</style>")
txtstream.WriteLine("</head>")
txtstream.WriteLine("<body>")
txtstream.WriteLine("<center>")
txtstream.WriteLine("</br>")
txtstream.WriteLine("<table style='border:Double;border-
width:1px;border-color:navy;' rules=all frames=both cellpadding=2
cellspacing=2 Width=0>")
txtstream.WriteLine("Response.Write(""<tr>"" & vbcrlf)")
For Each col as System.Data.DataColumn in ds.Tables(0).Columns
txtstream.WriteLine("Response.Write(""<th align='left'
nowrap='nowrap'>" & col.Caption & "</th>"" & vbcrlf)")
Next
txtstream.WriteLine("Response.Write(""</tr>"" & vbcrlf)")

for each row as System.Data.DataRow in ds.Tables(0).Rows
txtstream.WriteLine("Response.Write(""<tr>"" & vbcrlf)")
For Each col as System.Data.DataColumn in ds.Tables(0).Columns
txtstream.WriteLine("Response.Write(""<td  align='left'
nowrap='true'><span>" & row.Item(col.Caption) & "</span></td>""
& vbcrlf)")
Next

txtstream.WriteLine("Response.Write(""</tr>"" & vbcrlf)")

Next
txtstream.WriteLine("%>")
txtstream.WriteLine("</table>")
txtstream.WriteLine("</body>")
txtstream.WriteLine("</html>")
txtstream.Close()
```

```
Dim cnstr as String = "Provider=Microsoft.Jet.OLEDB.4.0;Data
Source=C:\NWIND.MDB"
Dim strQuery as String = "Select * From [Products]"

Dim cn As System.Data.OleDb.OleDbConnection = new
System.Data.OleDb.OleDbConnection(cnstr)
cn.Open()

Dim cmd As System.Data.OleDb.OleDbCommand = new
System.Data.OleDb.OleDbCommand()
cmd.Connection = cn
cmd.CommandType = 1
cmd.CommandText = strQuery
cmd.ExecuteNonquery()

Dim da As System.Data.OleDb.OleDbDataAdapter = new
System.Data.OleDb.OleDbDataAdapter(cmd)

Dim ds as new System.Data.DataSet
da.Fill(ds, "Products")

Dim ws As Object = CreateObject("WScript.Shell")
Dim fso As Object = CreateObject("Scripting.FileSystemObject")
Dim txtstream as Object = fso.OpenTextFile(ws.CurrentDirectory +
"\Products.aspx", 2, True, -2)
txtstream.WriteLine("<hmtl>")
txtstream.WriteLine("<head>")
txtstream.WriteLine("<title>Products</title>")
txtstream.WriteLine("<style type='text/css'>")
txtstream.WriteLine("th")
txtstream.WriteLine("{")
txtstream.WriteLine("    COLOR: darkred;")
txtstream.WriteLine("    BACKGROUND-COLOR: #eeeeee;")
```

```
txtstream.WriteLine("    FONT-FAMILY:font-family: Cambria, serif;")
txtstream.WriteLine("    FONT-SIZE: 12px;")
txtstream.WriteLine("    text-align: left;")
txtstream.WriteLine("    white-Space: nowrap='nowrap';")
txtstream.WriteLine("}")
txtstream.WriteLine("td")
txtstream.WriteLine("{")
txtstream.WriteLine("    COLOR: navy;")
txtstream.WriteLine("    BACKGROUND-COLOR: #eeeeee;")
txtstream.WriteLine("    FONT-FAMILY: font-family: Cambria, serif;")
txtstream.WriteLine("    FONT-SIZE: 12px;")
txtstream.WriteLine("    text-align: left;")
txtstream.WriteLine("    white-Space: nowrap='nowrap';")
txtstream.WriteLine("}")
txtstream.WriteLine("</style>")
txtstream.WriteLine("</head>")
txtstream.WriteLine("<body>")
txtstream.WriteLine("<center>")
txtstream.WriteLine("</br>")
txtstream.WriteLine("<table style='border:Double;border-width:1px;border-color:navy;' rules=all frames=both cellpadding=2 cellspacing=2 Width=0>")
For Each col as System.Data.DataColumn in ds.Tables(0).Columns
txtstream.WriteLine("Response.Write(""<tr><th align='left' nowrap='nowrap'>" & col.Caption & "</th>"" & vbcrlf)")
for each row as System.Data.DataRow in ds.Tables(0).Rows
txtstream.WriteLine("Response.Write(""<td  align='left' nowrap='nowrap'>" & row.Item(col.Caption) & "</td>"" & vbcrlf)")

Next
txtstream.WriteLine("Response.Write(""</tr>"" & vbcrlf)")
Next
txtstream.WriteLine("%>")
txtstream.WriteLine("</table>")
txtstream.WriteLine("</body>")
txtstream.WriteLine("</html>")
txtstream.Close()
```

HTA Examples

B ELOW ARE EXAMPLES OF OLEDB USING A DATASET.

Reports

   Horizontal

```
Dim cnstr as String = "Provider=Microsoft.Jet.OLEDB.4.0;Data
Source=C:\NWIND.MDB"
Dim strQuery as String = "Select * From [Products]"

Dim cn As System.Data.OleDb.OleDbConnection  = new
System.Data.OleDb.OleDbConnection(cnstr)
cn.Open()

Dim cmd As System.Data.OleDb.OleDbCommand  = new
System.Data.OleDb.OleDbCommand()
cmd.Connection = cn
cmd.CommandType = 1
cmd.CommandText = strQuery
cmd.ExecuteNonquery()

Dim da As System.Data.OleDb.OleDbDataAdapter  = new
System.Data.OleDb.OleDbDataAdapter(cmd)
```

```
Dim ds as new System.Data.DataSet
da.Fill(ds, "Products")

Dim ws As Object = CreateObject("WScript.Shell")
Dim fso As Object = CreateObject("Scripting.FileSystemObject")
Dim txtstream as Object = fso.OpenTextFile(ws.CurrentDirectory +
"\Products.hta", 2, True, -2)
txtstream.WriteLine("<hmtl>")
txtstream.WriteLine("<head>")
txtstream.WriteLine("<HTA:APPLICATION ")
txtstream.WriteLine("ID = 'Products' ")
txtstream.WriteLine("APPLICATIONNAME = 'Products' ")
txtstream.WriteLine("SCROLL = 'yes' ")
txtstream.WriteLine("SINGLEINSTANCE = 'yes' ")
txtstream.WriteLine("WINDOWSTATE = 'maximize' >")
txtstream.WriteLine("<title>Products</title>")
txtstream.WriteLine("<style type='text/css'>")
txtstream.WriteLine("th")
txtstream.WriteLine(" {")
txtstream.WriteLine("    COLOR: darkred;")
txtstream.WriteLine("    BACKGROUND-COLOR: #eeeeee;")
txtstream.WriteLine("    FONT-FAMILY:font-family: Cambria, serif;")
txtstream.WriteLine("    FONT-SIZE: 12px;")
txtstream.WriteLine("    text-align: left;")
txtstream.WriteLine("    white-Space: nowrap='nowrap';")
txtstream.WriteLine("}")
txtstream.WriteLine("td")
txtstream.WriteLine(" {")
txtstream.WriteLine("    COLOR: navy;")
txtstream.WriteLine("    BACKGROUND-COLOR: #eeeeee;")
txtstream.WriteLine("    FONT-FAMILY: font-family: Cambria, serif;")
txtstream.WriteLine("    FONT-SIZE: 12px;")
txtstream.WriteLine("    text-align: left;")
txtstream.WriteLine("    white-Space: nowrap='nowrap';")
txtstream.WriteLine("}")
txtstream.WriteLine("</style>")
```

```
txtstream.WriteLine("</head>")
txtstream.WriteLine("<body>")
txtstream.WriteLine("<center>")
txtstream.WriteLine("</br>")
txtstream.WriteLine("<table border=0 cellspacing=3 cellpadding=3>")
txtstream.WriteLine("<tr>")
For Each col as System.Data.DataColumn in ds.Tables(0).Columns
txtstream.WriteLine("<th align='left' nowrap='nowrap'>" & col.Caption
& "</th>")
Next
txtstream.WriteLine("</tr>")

for each row as System.Data.DataRow in ds.Tables(0).Rows
txtstream.WriteLine("<tr>")
For Each col as System.Data.DataColumn in ds.Tables(0).Columns
txtstream.WriteLine("<td  align='left' nowrap='nowrap'>" &
row.Item(col.Caption) & "</td>")
Next
txtstream.WriteLine("</tr>")

Next
txtstream.WriteLine("</table>")
txtstream.WriteLine("</body>")
txtstream.WriteLine("</html>")
txtstream.Close()
```

Vertical

```
Dim cnstr as String = "Provider=Microsoft.Jet.OLEDB.4.0;Data
Source=C:\NWIND.MDB"
Dim strQuery as String = "Select * From [Products]"
```

```
Dim cn As System.Data.OleDb.OleDbConnection = new
System.Data.OleDb.OleDbConnection(cnstr)
cn.Open()

Dim cmd As System.Data.OleDb.OleDbCommand = new
System.Data.OleDb.OleDbCommand()
cmd.Connection = cn
cmd.CommandType = 1
cmd.CommandText = strQuery
cmd.ExecuteNonquery()

Dim da As System.Data.OleDb.OleDbDataAdapter = new
System.Data.OleDb.OleDbDataAdapter(cmd)

Dim ds as new System.Data.DataSet
da.Fill(ds, "Products")

Dim ws As Object = CreateObject("WScript.Shell")
Dim fso As Object = CreateObject("Scripting.FileSystemObject")
Dim txtstream as Object = fso.OpenTextFile(ws.CurrentDirectory +
"\Products.hta", 2, True, -2)
txtstream.WriteLine("<hmtl>")
txtstream.WriteLine("<head>")
txtstream.WriteLine("<HTA:APPLICATION ")
txtstream.WriteLine("ID = 'Products' ")
txtstream.WriteLine("APPLICATIONNAME = 'Products' ")
txtstream.WriteLine("SCROLL = 'yes' ")
txtstream.WriteLine("SINGLEINSTANCE = 'yes' ")
txtstream.WriteLine("WINDOWSTATE = 'maximize' >")
txtstream.WriteLine("<title>Products</title>")
txtstream.WriteLine("<style type='text/css'>")
txtstream.WriteLine("th")
txtstream.WriteLine(" {")
txtstream.WriteLine("   COLOR: darkred;")
txtstream.WriteLine("   BACKGROUND-COLOR: #eeeeee;")
txtstream.WriteLine("   FONT-FAMILY:font-family: Cambria, serif;")
txtstream.WriteLine("   FONT-SIZE: 12px;")
```

```
txtstream.WriteLine("    text-align: left;")
txtstream.WriteLine("    white-Space: nowrap='nowrap';")
txtstream.WriteLine("}")
txtstream.WriteLine("td")
txtstream.WriteLine(" {")
txtstream.WriteLine("    COLOR: navy;")
txtstream.WriteLine("    BACKGROUND-COLOR: #eeeeee;")
txtstream.WriteLine("    FONT-FAMILY: font-family: Cambria, serif;")
txtstream.WriteLine("    FONT-SIZE: 12px;")
txtstream.WriteLine("    text-align: left;")
txtstream.WriteLine("    white-Space: nowrap='nowrap';")
txtstream.WriteLine("}")
txtstream.WriteLine("</style>")
txtstream.WriteLine("</head>")
txtstream.WriteLine("<body>")
txtstream.WriteLine("<center>")
txtstream.WriteLine("</br>")
txtstream.WriteLine("<table border=0 cellspacing=3 cellpadding=3>")
For Each col as System.Data.DataColumn in ds.Tables(0).Columns
txtstream.WriteLine("<tr><th align='left' nowrap='nowrap'>" &
col.Caption & "</th>")
for each row as System.Data.DataRow in ds.Tables(0).Rows
txtstream.WriteLine("<td  align='left' nowrap='nowrap'>" &
row.Item(col.Caption) & "</td>")

Next
txtstream.WriteLine("</tr>")
Next
txtstream.WriteLine("</table>")
txtstream.WriteLine("</body>")
txtstream.WriteLine("</html>")
txtstream.Close()
```

Tables

Horizontal

```
Dim cnstr as String = "Provider=Microsoft.Jet.OLEDB.4.0;Data
Source=C:\NWIND.MDB"
Dim strQuery as String = "Select * From [Products]"

Dim cn As System.Data.OleDb.OleDbConnection = new
System.Data.OleDb.OleDbConnection(cnstr)
cn.Open()

Dim cmd As System.Data.OleDb.OleDbCommand = new
System.Data.OleDb.OleDbCommand()
cmd.Connection = cn
cmd.CommandType = 1
cmd.CommandText = strQuery
cmd.ExecuteNonquery()

Dim da As System.Data.OleDb.OleDbDataAdapter = new
System.Data.OleDb.OleDbDataAdapter(cmd)

Dim ds as new System.Data.DataSet
da.Fill(ds, "Products")

Dim ws As Object = CreateObject("WScript.Shell")
Dim fso As Object = CreateObject("Scripting.FileSystemObject")
Dim txtstream as Object = fso.OpenTextFile(ws.CurrentDirectory +
"\Products.hta", 2, True, -2)
txtstream.WriteLine("<hmtl>")
txtstream.WriteLine("<head>")
txtstream.WriteLine("<HTA:APPLICATION ")
txtstream.WriteLine("ID = 'Products' ")
txtstream.WriteLine("APPLICATIONNAME = 'Products' ")
txtstream.WriteLine("SCROLL = 'yes' ")
txtstream.WriteLine("SINGLEINSTANCE = 'yes' ")
txtstream.WriteLine("WINDOWSTATE = 'maximize' >")
```

```
txtstream.WriteLine("<title>Products</title>")
txtstream.WriteLine("<style type='text/css'>")
txtstream.WriteLine("th")
txtstream.WriteLine("{")
txtstream.WriteLine("    COLOR: darkred;")
txtstream.WriteLine("    BACKGROUND-COLOR: #eeeeee;")
txtstream.WriteLine("    FONT-FAMILY:font-family: Cambria, serif;")
txtstream.WriteLine("    FONT-SIZE: 12px;")
txtstream.WriteLine("    text-align: left;")
txtstream.WriteLine("    white-Space: nowrap='nowrap';")
txtstream.WriteLine("}")
txtstream.WriteLine("td")
txtstream.WriteLine("{")
txtstream.WriteLine("    COLOR: navy;")
txtstream.WriteLine("    BACKGROUND-COLOR: #eeeeee;")
txtstream.WriteLine("    FONT-FAMILY: font-family: Cambria, serif;")
txtstream.WriteLine("    FONT-SIZE: 12px;")
txtstream.WriteLine("    text-align: left;")
txtstream.WriteLine("    white-Space: nowrap='nowrap';")
txtstream.WriteLine("}")
txtstream.WriteLine("</style>")
txtstream.WriteLine("</head>")
txtstream.WriteLine("<body>")
txtstream.WriteLine("<center>")
txtstream.WriteLine("</br>")
txtstream.WriteLine("<table style='border:Double;border-
width:1px;border-color:navy;' rules=all frames=both cellpadding=2
cellspacing=2 Width=0>")
txtstream.WriteLine("<tr>")
For Each col as System.Data.DataColumn in ds.Tables(0).Columns
txtstream.WriteLine("<th align='left' nowrap='nowrap'>" & col.Caption
& "</th>")
Next
txtstream.WriteLine("</tr>")

for each row as System.Data.DataRow in ds.Tables(0).Rows
txtstream.WriteLine("<tr>")
```

```vbnet
For Each col as System.Data.DataColumn in ds.Tables(0).Columns
    txtstream.WriteLine("<td  align='left' nowrap='nowrap'>" &
row.Item(col.Caption) & "</td>")
Next
txtstream.WriteLine("</tr>")

Next
txtstream.WriteLine("</table>")
txtstream.WriteLine("</body>")
txtstream.WriteLine("</html>")
txtstream.Close()
```

Vertical

```vbnet
Dim cnstr as String = "Provider=Microsoft.Jet.OLEDB.4.0;Data
Source=C:\NWIND.MDB"
Dim strQuery as String = "Select * From [Products]"

Dim cn As System.Data.OleDb.OleDbConnection  = new
System.Data.OleDb.OleDbConnection(cnstr)
cn.Open()

Dim cmd As System.Data.OleDb.OleDbCommand  = new
System.Data.OleDb.OleDbCommand()
cmd.Connection = cn
cmd.CommandType = 1
cmd.CommandText = strQuery
cmd.ExecuteNonquery()

Dim da As System.Data.OleDb.OleDbDataAdapter  = new
System.Data.OleDb.OleDbDataAdapter(cmd)
```

```
Dim ds as new System.Data.DataSet
da.Fill(ds, "Products")

Dim ws As Object = CreateObject("WScript.Shell")
Dim fso As Object = CreateObject("Scripting.FileSystemObject")
Dim txtstream as Object = fso.OpenTextFile(ws.CurrentDirectory +
"\Products.hta", 2, True, -2)
txtstream.WriteLine("<hmtl>")
txtstream.WriteLine("<head>")
txtstream.WriteLine("<HTA:APPLICATION ")
txtstream.WriteLine("ID = 'Products' ")
txtstream.WriteLine("APPLICATIONNAME = 'Products' ")
txtstream.WriteLine("SCROLL = 'yes' ")
txtstream.WriteLine("SINGLEINSTANCE = 'yes' ")
txtstream.WriteLine("WINDOWSTATE = 'maximize' >")
txtstream.WriteLine("<title>Products</title>")
txtstream.WriteLine("<style type='text/css'>")
txtstream.WriteLine("th")
txtstream.WriteLine(" {")
txtstream.WriteLine("    COLOR: darkred;")
txtstream.WriteLine("    BACKGROUND-COLOR: #eeeeee;")
txtstream.WriteLine("    FONT-FAMILY:font-family: Cambria, serif;")
txtstream.WriteLine("    FONT-SIZE: 12px;")
txtstream.WriteLine("    text-align: left;")
txtstream.WriteLine("    white-Space: nowrap='nowrap';")
txtstream.WriteLine("}")
txtstream.WriteLine("td")
txtstream.WriteLine(" {")
txtstream.WriteLine("    COLOR: navy;")
txtstream.WriteLine("    BACKGROUND-COLOR: #eeeeee;")
txtstream.WriteLine("    FONT-FAMILY: font-family: Cambria, serif;")
txtstream.WriteLine("    FONT-SIZE: 12px;")
txtstream.WriteLine("    text-align: left;")
txtstream.WriteLine("    white-Space: nowrap='nowrap';")
txtstream.WriteLine("}")
txtstream.WriteLine("</style>")
txtstream.WriteLine("</head>")
```

```
txtstream.WriteLine("<body>")
txtstream.WriteLine("<center>")
txtstream.WriteLine("</br>")
txtstream.WriteLine("<table style='border:Double;border-
width:1px;border-color:navy;' rules=all frames=both cellpadding=2
cellspacing=2 Width=0>")
For Each col as System.Data.DataColumn in ds.Tables(0).Columns
txtstream.WriteLine("<tr><th align='left' nowrap='nowrap'>" &
col.Caption & "</th>")
for each row as System.Data.DataRow in ds.Tables(0).Rows
txtstream.WriteLine("<td  align='left' nowrap='nowrap'>" &
row.Item(col.Caption) & "</td>")

Next
txtstream.WriteLine("</tr>")
Next
txtstream.WriteLine("</table>")
txtstream.WriteLine("</body>")
txtstream.WriteLine("</html>")
txtstream.Close()
```

HTML Examples

BELOW ARE EXAMPLES OF OLEDB USING A DATASET.

Reports

    Horizontal

```
Dim cnstr as String = "Provider=Microsoft.Jet.OLEDB.4.0;Data
Source=C:\NWIND.MDB"
Dim strQuery as String = "Select * From [Products]"

Dim cn As System.Data.OleDb.OleDbConnection  = new
System.Data.OleDb.OleDbConnection(cnstr)
cn.Open()

Dim cmd As System.Data.OleDb.OleDbCommand  = new
System.Data.OleDb.OleDbCommand()
cmd.Connection = cn
cmd.CommandType = 1
cmd.CommandText = strQuery
cmd.ExecuteNonquery()
```

```
Dim da As System.Data.OleDb.OleDbDataAdapter = new
System.Data.OleDb.OleDbDataAdapter(cmd)

Dim ds as new System.Data.DataSet
da.Fill(ds, "Products")

Dim ws As Object = CreateObject("WScript.Shell")
Dim fso As Object = CreateObject("Scripting.FileSystemObject")
Dim txtstream as Object = fso.OpenTextFile(ws.CurrentDirectory +
"\Products.html", 2, True, -2)
txtstream.WriteLine("<hmtl>")
txtstream.WriteLine("<head>")
txtstream.WriteLine("<title>Products</title>")
txtstream.WriteLine("<style type='text/css'>")
txtstream.WriteLine("th")
txtstream.WriteLine(" {")
txtstream.WriteLine("    COLOR: darkred;")
txtstream.WriteLine("    BACKGROUND-COLOR: #eeeeee;")
txtstream.WriteLine("    FONT-FAMILY:font-family: Cambria, serif;")
txtstream.WriteLine("    FONT-SIZE: 12px;")
txtstream.WriteLine("    text-align: left;")
txtstream.WriteLine("    white-Space: nowrap='nowrap';")
txtstream.WriteLine("}")
txtstream.WriteLine("td")
txtstream.WriteLine(" {")
txtstream.WriteLine("    COLOR: navy;")
txtstream.WriteLine("    BACKGROUND-COLOR: #eeeeee;")
txtstream.WriteLine("    FONT-FAMILY: font-family: Cambria, serif;")
txtstream.WriteLine("    FONT-SIZE: 12px;")
txtstream.WriteLine("    text-align: left;")
txtstream.WriteLine("    white-Space: nowrap='nowrap';")
txtstream.WriteLine("}")
txtstream.WriteLine("</style>")
txtstream.WriteLine("</head>")
txtstream.WriteLine("<body>")
txtstream.WriteLine("<center>")
txtstream.WriteLine("</br>")
```

```
txtstream.WriteLine("<table border=0 cellspacing=3 cellpadding=3>")
txtstream.WriteLine("<tr>")
For Each col as System.Data.DataColumn in ds.Tables(0).Columns
txtstream.WriteLine("<th align='left' nowrap='nowrap'>" & col.Caption
& "</th>")
Next
txtstream.WriteLine("</tr>")

for each row as System.Data.DataRow in ds.Tables(0).Rows
txtstream.WriteLine("<tr>")
For Each col as System.Data.DataColumn in ds.Tables(0).Columns
txtstream.WriteLine("<td  align='left' nowrap='nowrap'>" &
row.Item(col.Caption) & "</td>")
Next
txtstream.WriteLine("</tr>")

Next
txtstream.WriteLine("</table>")
txtstream.WriteLine("</body>")
txtstream.WriteLine("</html>")
txtstream.Close()


    Vertical


Dim cnstr as String = "Provider=Microsoft.Jet.OLEDB.4.0;Data
Source=C:\NWIND.MDB"
Dim strQuery as String = "Select * From [Products]"

Dim cn As System.Data.OleDb.OleDbConnection  = new
System.Data.OleDb.OleDbConnection(cnstr)
cn.Open()

Dim cmd As System.Data.OleDb.OleDbCommand  = new
System.Data.OleDb.OleDbCommand()
cmd.Connection = cn
```

```
cmd.CommandType = 1
cmd.CommandText = strQuery
cmd.ExecuteNonquery()

Dim da As System.Data.OleDb.OleDbDataAdapter = new
System.Data.OleDb.OleDbDataAdapter(cmd)

Dim ds as new System.Data.DataSet
da.Fill(ds, "Products")

Dim ws As Object = CreateObject("WScript.Shell")
Dim fso As Object = CreateObject("Scripting.FileSystemObject")
Dim txtstream as Object = fso.OpenTextFile(ws.CurrentDirectory +
"\Products.html", 2, True, -2)
txtstream.WriteLine("<hmtl>")
txtstream.WriteLine("<head>")
txtstream.WriteLine("<title>Products</title>")
txtstream.WriteLine("<style type='text/css'>")
txtstream.WriteLine("th")
txtstream.WriteLine("{")
txtstream.WriteLine("    COLOR: darkred;")
txtstream.WriteLine("    BACKGROUND-COLOR: #eeeeee;")
txtstream.WriteLine("    FONT-FAMILY:font-family: Cambria, serif;")
txtstream.WriteLine("    FONT-SIZE: 12px;")
txtstream.WriteLine("    text-align: left;")
txtstream.WriteLine("    white-Space: nowrap='nowrap';")
txtstream.WriteLine("}")
txtstream.WriteLine("td")
txtstream.WriteLine("{")
txtstream.WriteLine("    COLOR: navy;")
txtstream.WriteLine("    BACKGROUND-COLOR: #eeeeee;")
txtstream.WriteLine("    FONT-FAMILY: font-family: Cambria, serif;")
txtstream.WriteLine("    FONT-SIZE: 12px;")
txtstream.WriteLine("    text-align: left;")
txtstream.WriteLine("    white-Space: nowrap='nowrap';")
txtstream.WriteLine("}")
txtstream.WriteLine("</style>")
```

```
txtstream.WriteLine("</head>")
txtstream.WriteLine("<body>")
txtstream.WriteLine("<center>")
txtstream.WriteLine("</br>")
txtstream.WriteLine("</br>")
txtstream.WriteLine("<table border=0 cellspacing=3 cellpadding=3>")
For Each col as System.Data.DataColumn in ds.Tables(0).Columns
txtstream.WriteLine("<tr><th align='left' nowrap='nowrap'>" &
col.Caption & "</th>")
for each row as System.Data.DataRow in ds.Tables(0).Rows
txtstream.WriteLine("<td  align='left' nowrap='nowrap'>" &
row.Item(col.Caption) & "</td>")

Next
txtstream.WriteLine("</tr>")
Next
txtstream.WriteLine("</table>")
txtstream.WriteLine("</body>")
txtstream.WriteLine("</html>")
txtstream.Close()
```

Tables

    Horizontal

```
Dim cnstr as String = "Provider=Microsoft.Jet.OLEDB.4.0;Data
Source=C:\NWIND.MDB"
Dim strQuery as String = "Select * From [Products]"

Dim cn As System.Data.OleDb.OleDbConnection  = new
System.Data.OleDb.OleDbConnection(cnstr)
```

```
cn.Open()

Dim cmd As System.Data.OleDb.OleDbCommand = new
System.Data.OleDb.OleDbCommand()
cmd.Connection = cn
cmd.CommandType = 1
cmd.CommandText = strQuery
cmd.ExecuteNonquery()

Dim da As System.Data.OleDb.OleDbDataAdapter = new
System.Data.OleDb.OleDbDataAdapter(cmd)

Dim ds as new System.Data.DataSet
da.Fill(ds, "Products")

Dim ws As Object = CreateObject("WScript.Shell")
Dim fso As Object = CreateObject("Scripting.FileSystemObject")
Dim txtstream as Object = fso.OpenTextFile(ws.CurrentDirectory +
"\Products.html", 2, True, -2)
txtstream.WriteLine("<hmtl>")
txtstream.WriteLine("<head>")
txtstream.WriteLine("<title>Products</title>")
txtstream.WriteLine("<style type='text/css'>")
txtstream.WriteLine("th")
txtstream.WriteLine(" {")
txtstream.WriteLine("   COLOR: darkred;")
txtstream.WriteLine("   BACKGROUND-COLOR: #eeeeee;")
txtstream.WriteLine("   FONT-FAMILY:font-family: Cambria, serif;")
txtstream.WriteLine("   FONT-SIZE: 12px;")
txtstream.WriteLine("   text-align: left;")
txtstream.WriteLine("   white-Space: nowrap='nowrap';")
txtstream.WriteLine("}")
txtstream.WriteLine("td")
txtstream.WriteLine(" {")
txtstream.WriteLine("   COLOR: navy;")
txtstream.WriteLine("   BACKGROUND-COLOR: #eeeeee;")
txtstream.WriteLine("   FONT-FAMILY: font-family: Cambria, serif;")
```

```
txtstream.WriteLine("    FONT-SIZE: 12px;")
txtstream.WriteLine("    text-align: left;")
txtstream.WriteLine("    white-Space: nowrap='nowrap';")
txtstream.WriteLine("}")
txtstream.WriteLine("</style>")
txtstream.WriteLine("</head>")
txtstream.WriteLine("<body>")
txtstream.WriteLine("<center>")
txtstream.WriteLine("</br>")
txtstream.WriteLine("<table style='border:Double;border-
width:1px;border-color:navy;' rules=all frames=both cellpadding=2
cellspacing=2 Width=0>")
txtstream.WriteLine("<tr>")
For Each col as System.Data.DataColumn in ds.Tables(0).Columns
txtstream.WriteLine("<th align='left' nowrap='nowrap'>" & col.Caption
& "</th>")
Next
txtstream.WriteLine("</tr>")

for each row as System.Data.DataRow in ds.Tables(0).Rows
txtstream.WriteLine("<tr>")
For Each col as System.Data.DataColumn in ds.Tables(0).Columns
txtstream.WriteLine("<td  align='left' nowrap='nowrap'>" &
row.Item(col.Caption) & "</td>")
Next
txtstream.WriteLine("</tr>")

Next
txtstream.WriteLine("</table>")
txtstream.WriteLine("</body>")
txtstream.WriteLine("</html>")
txtstream.Close()
```

Vertical

```
Dim cnstr as String = "Provider=Microsoft.Jet.OLEDB.4.0;Data
Source=C:\NWIND.MDB"
Dim strQuery as String = "Select * From [Products]"

Dim cn As System.Data.OleDb.OleDbConnection = new
System.Data.OleDb.OleDbConnection(cnstr)
cn.Open()

Dim cmd As System.Data.OleDb.OleDbCommand = new
System.Data.OleDb.OleDbCommand()
cmd.Connection = cn
cmd.CommandType = 1
cmd.CommandText = strQuery
cmd.ExecuteNonquery()

Dim da As System.Data.OleDb.OleDbDataAdapter = new
System.Data.OleDb.OleDbDataAdapter(cmd)

Dim ds as new System.Data.DataSet
da.Fill(ds, "Products")

Dim ws As Object = CreateObject("WScript.Shell")
Dim fso As Object = CreateObject("Scripting.FileSystemObject")
Dim txtstream as Object = fso.OpenTextFile(ws.CurrentDirectory +
"\Products.html", 2, True, -2)
txtstream.WriteLine("<hmtl>")
txtstream.WriteLine("<head>")
txtstream.WriteLine("<title>Products</title>")
txtstream.WriteLine("<style type='text/css'>")
txtstream.WriteLine("th")
txtstream.WriteLine("{")
txtstream.WriteLine("   COLOR: darkred;")
txtstream.WriteLine("   BACKGROUND-COLOR: #eeeeee;")
txtstream.WriteLine("   FONT-FAMILY:font-family: Cambria, serif;")
txtstream.WriteLine("   FONT-SIZE: 12px;")
txtstream.WriteLine("   text-align: left;")
```

```
txtstream.WriteLine("    white-Space: nowrap='nowrap';")
txtstream.WriteLine("}")
txtstream.WriteLine("td")
txtstream.WriteLine("{")
txtstream.WriteLine("    COLOR: navy;")
txtstream.WriteLine("    BACKGROUND-COLOR: #eeeeee;")
txtstream.WriteLine("    FONT-FAMILY: font-family: Cambria, serif;")
txtstream.WriteLine("    FONT-SIZE: 12px;")
txtstream.WriteLine("    text-align: left;")
txtstream.WriteLine("    white-Space: nowrap='nowrap';")
txtstream.WriteLine("}")
txtstream.WriteLine("</style>")
txtstream.WriteLine("</head>")
txtstream.WriteLine("<body>")
txtstream.WriteLine("<center>")
txtstream.WriteLine("</br>")
txtstream.WriteLine("<table style='border:Double;border-
width:1px;border-color:navy;' rules=all frames=both cellpadding=2
cellspacing=2 Width=0>")
For Each col as System.Data.DataColumn in ds.Tables(0).Columns
txtstream.WriteLine("<tr><th align='left' nowrap='nowrap'>" &
col.Caption & "</th>")
for each row as System.Data.DataRow in ds.Tables(0).Rows
txtstream.WriteLine("<td  align='left' nowrap='nowrap'>" &
row.Item(col.Caption) & "</td>")

Next
txtstream.WriteLine("</tr>")
Next
txtstream.WriteLine("</table>")
txtstream.WriteLine("</body>")
txtstream.WriteLine("</html>")
txtstream.Close()
```

Excel Examples

B ELOW ARE EXAMPLES OF OLEDB USING A DATASET.

Excel Automation

   Horizontal

Excel Spreadsheet

Horizontal

```
Dim cnstr as String = "Provider=Microsoft.Jet.OLEDB.4.0;Data
Source=C:\NWIND.MDB"
Dim strQuery as String = "Select * From [Products]"

Dim cn As System.Data.OleDb.OleDbConnection  = new
System.Data.OleDb.OleDbConnection(cnstr)
cn.Open()

Dim cmd As System.Data.OleDb.OleDbCommand  = new
System.Data.OleDb.OleDbCommand()
cmd.Connection = cn
cmd.CommandType = 1
cmd.CommandText = strQuery
cmd.ExecuteNonquery()
```

```
Dim da As System.Data.OleDb.OleDbDataAdapter = new
System.Data.OleDb.OleDbDataAdapter(cmd)

Dim ds as new System.Data.DataSet
da.Fill(ds, "Products")

Dim ws As Object = createObject("WScript.Shell")
Dim cdir As String = ws.CurrentDirectory + "\Products.xml"
Dim fso As Object = CreateObject("Scripting.FileSystemObject")
Dim txtstream As Object = fso.OpenTextFile(cdir, 2, true, -2)
txtstream.WriteLine("<?xml version=""1.0""?>")
txtstream.WriteLine("<?mso-application progid=""Excel.Sheet""?>")
txtstream.WriteLine("<Workbook xmlns=""urn:schemas-microsoft-
com:office:spreadsheet"" xmlns:o=""urn:schemas-microsoft-
com:office:office"" xmlns:x=""urn:schemas-microsoft-com:office:excel""
xmlns:ss=""urn:schemas-microsoft-com:office:spreadsheet""
xmlns:html=""http://www.w3.org/TR/REC-html40"">")
txtstream.WriteLine("  <ExcelWorkbook xmlns=""urn:schemas-
microsoft-com:office:excel"">")
txtstream.WriteLine("    <WindowHeight>11835</WindowHeight>")
txtstream.WriteLine("    <WindowWidth>18960</WindowWidth>")
txtstream.WriteLine("    <WindowTopX>120</WindowTopX>")
txtstream.WriteLine("    <WindowTopY>135</WindowTopY>")
txtstream.WriteLine("    <ProtectStructure>False</ProtectStructure>")
txtstream.WriteLine("
<ProtectWindows>False</ProtectWindows>")
txtstream.WriteLine("  </ExcelWorkbook>")
txtstream.WriteLine("  <Styles>")
txtstream.WriteLine("        <Style ss:ID=""s62"">")
txtstream.WriteLine("            <Borders/>")
txtstream.WriteLine("            <Font ss:FontName=""Calibri""
x:Family=""Swiss"" ss:Size=""11"" ss:Color=""#000000""
ss:Bold=""1""/>")
txtstream.WriteLine("        </Style>")
txtstream.WriteLine("        <Style ss:ID=""s63"">")
txtstream.WriteLine("            <Alignment
ss:Horizontal=""Left"" ss:Vertical=""Bottom"" ss:Indent=""2""/>")
```

```
txtstream.WriteLine("                            <Font
ss:FontName="""Verdana""" x:Family="""Swiss""" ss:Size="""7.7"""
ss:Color="""#000000"""/>")
txtstream.WriteLine("          </Style>")
txtstream.WriteLine("  </Styles>")
txtstream.WriteLine("  <Worksheet
ss:Name="""Win32_NetworkAdapter""">")
txtstream.WriteLine("    <Table x:FullColumns="""1""" x:FullRows="""1"""
ss:DefaultRowHeight="""24.9375""">")
txtstream.WriteLine("      <Column ss:AutoFitWidth="""1"""
ss:Width="""82.5""" ss:Span="""5"""/>")
txtstream.WriteLine("      <Row ss:AutoFitHeight="""0""">")
foreach(col in ds.Tables(0).Columns)
txtstream.WriteLine("          <Cell ss:StyleID="""s62"""><Data
ss:Type="""String""">" + col.Caption + "</Data></Cell>")
Next
txtstream.WriteLine("      </Row>")
for each(row in ds.Tables(0).Rows)
txtstream.WriteLine("      <Row ss:AutoFitHeight="""0""">")
foreach(col in ds.Tables(0).Columns)
txtstream.WriteLine("          <Cell ss:StyleID="""s63"""><Data
ss:Type="""String""">" + row.Item(col.Caption) + "</Data></Cell>")
Next
txtstream.WriteLine("      </Row>")
Next
txtstream.WriteLine("    </Table>")
txtstream.WriteLine("  </Worksheet>")
txtstream.WriteLine("</Workbook>")
$iret = txtstream.Close()
```

Vertical

```
Dim cnstr as String = "Provider=Microsoft.Jet.OLEDB.4.0;Data
Source=C:\NWIND.MDB"
```

```vb
Dim strQuery as String = "Select * From [Products]"

Dim cn As System.Data.OleDb.OleDbConnection = new
System.Data.OleDb.OleDbConnection(cnstr)
cn.Open()

Dim cmd As System.Data.OleDb.OleDbCommand = new
System.Data.OleDb.OleDbCommand()
cmd.Connection = cn
cmd.CommandType = 1
cmd.CommandText = strQuery
cmd.ExecuteNonquery()

Dim da As System.Data.OleDb.OleDbDataAdapter = new
System.Data.OleDb.OleDbDataAdapter(cmd)

Dim ds as new System.Data.DataSet
da.Fill(ds, "Products")

Dim ws As Object = createObject("WScript.Shell")
Dim cdir As String = ws.CurrentDirectory + "\Products.xml"
Dim fso As Object = CreateObject("Scripting.FileSystemObject")
Dim txtstream As Object = fso.OpenTextFile(cdir, 2, true, -2)
txtstream.WriteLine("<?xml version=""1.0""?>")
txtstream.WriteLine("<?mso-application progid=""Excel.Sheet""?>")
txtstream.WriteLine("<Workbook xmlns=""urn:schemas-microsoft-
com:office:spreadsheet"" xmlns:o=""urn:schemas-microsoft-
com:office:office"" xmlns:x=""urn:schemas-microsoft-com:office:excel""
xmlns:ss=""urn:schemas-microsoft-com:office:spreadsheet""
xmlns:html=""http://www.w3.org/TR/REC-html40"">")
txtstream.WriteLine(" <ExcelWorkbook xmlns=""urn:schemas-
microsoft-com:office:excel"">")
txtstream.WriteLine("    <WindowHeight>11835</WindowHeight>")
txtstream.WriteLine("    <WindowWidth>18960</WindowWidth>")
txtstream.WriteLine("    <WindowTopX>120</WindowTopX>")
txtstream.WriteLine("    <WindowTopY>135</WindowTopY>")
txtstream.WriteLine("    <ProtectStructure>False</ProtectStructure>")
```

```vb
txtstream.WriteLine("
<ProtectWindows>False</ProtectWindows>")
txtstream.WriteLine(" </ExcelWorkbook>")
txtstream.WriteLine(" <Styles>")
txtstream.WriteLine("          <Style ss:ID=""s62"">")
txtstream.WriteLine("                <Borders/>")
txtstream.WriteLine("                <Font ss:FontName=""Calibri""
x:Family=""Swiss"" ss:Size=""11"" ss:Color=""#000000""
ss:Bold=""1""/>")
txtstream.WriteLine("          </Style>")
txtstream.WriteLine("          <Style ss:ID=""s63"">")
txtstream.WriteLine("                <Alignment
ss:Horizontal=""Left"" ss:Vertical=""Bottom"" ss:Indent=""2""/>")
txtstream.WriteLine("                <Font
ss:FontName=""Verdana"" x:Family=""Swiss"" ss:Size=""7.7""
ss:Color=""#000000""/>")
txtstream.WriteLine("          </Style>")
txtstream.WriteLine(" </Styles>")
txtstream.WriteLine(" <Worksheet
ss:Name=""Win32_NetworkAdapter"">")
txtstream.WriteLine("   <Table x:FullColumns=""1"" x:FullRows=""1""
ss:DefaultRowHeight=""24.9375"">")
txtstream.WriteLine("     <Column ss:AutoFitWidth=""1""
ss:Width=""82.5"" ss:Span=""5""/>")
txtstream.WriteLine("     <Row ss:AutoFitHeight=""0"">")
foreach(col in ds.Tables(0).Columns)
txtstream.WriteLine("        <Cell ss:StyleID=""s62""><Data
ss:Type=""String"">" + col.Caption + "</Data></Cell>")
Next
txtstream.WriteLine("     </Row>")
for each(row in ds.Tables(0).Rows)
txtstream.WriteLine("     <Row ss:AutoFitHeight=""0"">")
foreach(col in ds.Tables(0).Columns)
txtstream.WriteLine("        <Cell ss:StyleID=""s63""><Data
ss:Type=""String"">" + row.Item(col.Caption) + "</Data></Cell>")
Next
txtstream.WriteLine("     </Row>")
```

```
Next
txtstream.WriteLine("   </Table>")
txtstream.WriteLine("  </Worksheet>")
txtstream.WriteLine("</Workbook>")
$iret = txtstream.Close()
```

Using A CSV File

Horizontal

```
Dim cnstr as String = "Provider=Microsoft.Jet.OLEDB.4.0;Data
Source=C:\NWIND.MDB"
Dim strQuery as String = "Select * From [Products]"

Dim cn As System.Data.OleDb.OleDbConnection = new
System.Data.OleDb.OleDbConnection(cnstr)
cn.Open()

Dim cmd As System.Data.OleDb.OleDbCommand = new
System.Data.OleDb.OleDbCommand()
cmd.Connection = cn
cmd.CommandType = 1
cmd.CommandText = strQuery
cmd.ExecuteNonquery()

Dim da As System.Data.OleDb.OleDbDataAdapter = new
System.Data.OleDb.OleDbDataAdapter(cmd)

Dim ds as new System.Data.DataSet
da.Fill(ds, "Products")

Dim ws As Object = CreateObject("WScript.Shell")
Dim fso As Object = CreateObject("Scripting.FileSystemObject")
```

```
Dim txtstream as Object = fso.OpenTextFile(ws.CurrentDirectory +
"\Products.csv", 2, True, -2)
Dim tstr
tstr= ""
For Each col as System.Data.DataColumn in ds.Tables(0).Columns
If (tstr <> "") Then
tstr = tstr + ","
End If
tstr = tstr + col.Caption
Next
txtstream.Writeline(tstr)
tstr = ""

for each row as System.Data.DataRow in ds.Tables(0).Rows
For Each col as System.Data.DataColumn in ds.Tables(0).Columns
If (tstr <> "") Then
tstr = tstr + ","
End If
tstr = tstr & chr(34) & row.Item(col.Caption) & chr(34)
Next
txtstream.Writeline(tstr)
tstr = ""

Next

txtstream.Close

ws.Run(ws.CurrentDirectory + "\Products.csv")
```

Vertical

```
Dim cnstr as String = "Provider=Microsoft.Jet.OLEDB.4.0;Data
Source=C:\NWIND.MDB"
Dim strQuery as String = "Select * From [Products]"
```

```
Dim cn As System.Data.OleDb.OleDbConnection  = new
System.Data.OleDb.OleDbConnection(cnstr)
cn.Open()

Dim cmd As System.Data.OleDb.OleDbCommand  = new
System.Data.OleDb.OleDbCommand()
cmd.Connection = cn
cmd.CommandType = 1
cmd.CommandText = strQuery
cmd.ExecuteNonquery()

Dim da As System.Data.OleDb.OleDbDataAdapter  = new
System.Data.OleDb.OleDbDataAdapter(cmd)

Dim ds as new System.Data.DataSet
da.Fill(ds, "Products")

Dim ws As Object  = CreateObject("WScript.Shell")
Dim fso As Object  = CreateObject("Scripting.FileSystemObject")
Dim txtstream as Object  = fso.OpenTextFile(ws.CurrentDirectory +
"\Products.csv", 2, True, -2)
Dim tstr
tstr= ""
For Each col as System.Data.DataColumn in ds.Tables(0).Columns
tstr = col.Caption
for each row as System.Data.DataRow in ds.Tables(0).Rows
If (tstr <> "") Then
tstr = tstr + ","
End If
tstr = tstr & chr(34) & row.Item(col.Caption) & chr(34)

Next
txtstream.Writeline(tstr)
tstr = ""
Next
```

```
txtstream.Close

ws.Run(ws.CurrentDirectory + "\Products.csv")
```

Delimited Text Examples

BELOW ARE EXAMPLES OF OLEDB USING A DATASET.

Colon Delimited

Horizontal

```
Dim cnstr as String = "Provider=Microsoft.Jet.OLEDB.4.0;Data
Source=C:\NWIND.MDB"
Dim strQuery as String = "Select * From [Products]"

Dim cn As System.Data.OleDb.OleDbConnection  = new
System.Data.OleDb.OleDbConnection(cnstr)
cn.Open()

Dim cmd As System.Data.OleDb.OleDbCommand  = new
System.Data.OleDb.OleDbCommand()
cmd.Connection = cn
cmd.CommandType = 1
cmd.CommandText = strQuery
cmd.ExecuteNonquery()
```

```
Dim da As System.Data.OleDb.OleDbDataAdapter = new
System.Data.OleDb.OleDbDataAdapter(cmd)

Dim ds as new System.Data.DataSet
da.Fill(ds, "Products")

Dim ws As Object = CreateObject("WScript.Shell")
Dim fso As Object = CreateObject("Scripting.FileSystemObject")
Dim txtstream as Object = fso.OpenTextFile(ws.CurrentDirectory +
"\Products.txt", 2, True, -2)
Dim tstr
tstr= ""
For Each col as System.Data.DataColumn in ds.Tables(0).Columns
tstr = col.Caption
for each row as System.Data.DataRow in ds.Tables(0).Rows
If (tstr <> "") Then
tstr = tstr + ":"
End If
tstr = tstr & chr(34) & row.Item(col.Caption) & chr(34)

Next
txtstream.Writeline(tstr)
tstr = ""
Next

txtstream.Close
```

Vertical

```
Dim cnstr as String = "Provider=Microsoft.Jet.OLEDB.4.0;Data
Source=C:\NWIND.MDB"
Dim strQuery as String = "Select * From [Products]"

Dim cn As System.Data.OleDb.OleDbConnection = new
System.Data.OleDb.OleDbConnection(cnstr)
cn.Open()
```

```
Dim cmd As System.Data.OleDb.OleDbCommand = new
System.Data.OleDb.OleDbCommand()
cmd.Connection = cn
cmd.CommandType = 1
cmd.CommandText = strQuery
cmd.ExecuteNonquery()

Dim da As System.Data.OleDb.OleDbDataAdapter = new
System.Data.OleDb.OleDbDataAdapter(cmd)

Dim ds as new System.Data.DataSet
da.Fill(ds, "Products")

Dim ws As Object = CreateObject("WScript.Shell")
Dim fso As Object = CreateObject("Scripting.FileSystemObject")
Dim txtstream as Object = fso.OpenTextFile(ws.CurrentDirectory +
"\Products.txt", 2, True, -2)
Dim tstr
tstr= ""
For Each col as System.Data.DataColumn in ds.Tables(0).Columns
tstr = col.Caption
for each row as System.Data.DataRow in ds.Tables(0).Rows
If (tstr <> "") Then
tstr = tstr + ":"
End If
tstr = tstr & chr(34) & row.Item(col.Caption) & chr(34)

Next
txtstream.Writeline(tstr)
tstr = ""
Next

txtstream.Close
```

CSV

Horizontal


```
Dim cnstr as String = "Provider=Microsoft.Jet.OLEDB.4.0;Data
Source=C:\NWIND.MDB"
Dim strQuery as String = "Select * From [Products]"

Dim cn As System.Data.OleDb.OleDbConnection = new
System.Data.OleDb.OleDbConnection(cnstr)
cn.Open()

Dim cmd As System.Data.OleDb.OleDbCommand = new
System.Data.OleDb.OleDbCommand()
cmd.Connection = cn
cmd.CommandType = 1
cmd.CommandText = strQuery
cmd.ExecuteNonquery()

Dim da As System.Data.OleDb.OleDbDataAdapter = new
System.Data.OleDb.OleDbDataAdapter(cmd)

Dim ds as new System.Data.DataSet
da.Fill(ds, "Products")

Dim ws As Object = CreateObject("WScript.Shell")
Dim fso As Object = CreateObject("Scripting.FileSystemObject")
Dim txtstream as Object = fso.OpenTextFile(ws.CurrentDirectory +
"\Products.csv", 2, True, -2)
Dim tstr
tstr= ""
For Each col as System.Data.DataColumn in ds.Tables(0).Columns
If (tstr <> "") Then
tstr = tstr + ","
```

```
End If
tstr = tstr + col.Caption
Next
txtstream.Writeline(tstr)
tstr = ""

for each row as System.Data.DataRow in ds.Tables(0).Rows
For Each col as System.Data.DataColumn in ds.Tables(0).Columns
If (tstr <> "") Then
tstr = tstr + ","
End If
tstr = tstr & chr(34) & row.Item(col.Caption) & chr(34)
Next
txtstream.Writeline(tstr)
tstr = ""

Next

txtstream.Close
```

Vertical

```
Dim cnstr as String = "Provider=Microsoft.Jet.OLEDB.4.0;Data
Source=C:\NWIND.MDB"
Dim strQuery as String = "Select * From [Products]"

Dim cn As System.Data.OleDb.OleDbConnection  = new
System.Data.OleDb.OleDbConnection(cnstr)
cn.Open()

Dim cmd As System.Data.OleDb.OleDbCommand  = new
System.Data.OleDb.OleDbCommand()
cmd.Connection = cn
cmd.CommandType = 1
cmd.CommandText = strQuery
cmd.ExecuteNonquery()
```

```vbnet
Dim da As System.Data.OleDb.OleDbDataAdapter = new
System.Data.OleDb.OleDbDataAdapter(cmd)

Dim ds as new System.Data.DataSet
da.Fill(ds, "Products")

Dim ws As Object = CreateObject("WScript.Shell")
Dim fso As Object = CreateObject("Scripting.FileSystemObject")
Dim txtstream as Object = fso.OpenTextFile(ws.CurrentDirectory +
"\Products.csv", 2, True, -2)
Dim tstr
tstr= ""
For Each col as System.Data.DataColumn in ds.Tables(0).Columns
tstr = col.Caption
for each row as System.Data.DataRow in ds.Tables(0).Rows
If (tstr <> "") Then
tstr = tstr + ","
End If
tstr = tstr & chr(34) & row.Item(col.Caption) & chr(34)

Next
txtstream.Writeline(tstr)
tstr = ""
Next

txtstream.Close


Exclamation

Horizontal


Dim cnstr as String = "Provider=Microsoft.Jet.OLEDB.4.0;Data
Source=C:\NWIND.MDB"
Dim strQuery as String = "Select * From [Products]"
```

```vb
Dim cn As System.Data.OleDb.OleDbConnection = new
System.Data.OleDb.OleDbConnection(cnstr)
cn.Open()

Dim cmd As System.Data.OleDb.OleDbCommand = new
System.Data.OleDb.OleDbCommand()
cmd.Connection = cn
cmd.CommandType = 1
cmd.CommandText = strQuery
cmd.ExecuteNonquery()

Dim da As System.Data.OleDb.OleDbDataAdapter = new
System.Data.OleDb.OleDbDataAdapter(cmd)

Dim ds as new System.Data.DataSet
da.Fill(ds, "Products")

Dim ws As Object = CreateObject("WScript.Shell")
Dim fso As Object = CreateObject("Scripting.FileSystemObject")
Dim txtstream as Object = fso.OpenTextFile(ws.CurrentDirectory +
"\Products.txt", 2, True, -2)
Dim tstr
tstr= ""
For Each col as System.Data.DataColumn in ds.Tables(0).Columns
If (tstr <> "") Then
tstr = tstr + "!"
End If
tstr = tstr + col.Caption
Next
txtstream.Writeline(tstr)
tstr = ""

for each row as System.Data.DataRow in ds.Tables(0).Rows
For Each col as System.Data.DataColumn in ds.Tables(0).Columns
If (tstr <> "") Then
tstr = tstr + "!"
```

```
End If
tstr = tstr & chr(34) & row.Item(col.Caption) & chr(34)
Next
txtstream.Writeline(tstr)
tstr = ""

Next

txtstream.Close
```

Vertical


```
Dim cnstr as String = "Provider=Microsoft.Jet.OLEDB.4.0;Data
Source=C:\NWIND.MDB"
Dim strQuery as String = "Select * From [Products]"

Dim cn As System.Data.OleDb.OleDbConnection  = new
System.Data.OleDb.OleDbConnection(cnstr)
cn.Open()

Dim cmd As System.Data.OleDb.OleDbCommand  = new
System.Data.OleDb.OleDbCommand()
cmd.Connection = cn
cmd.CommandType = 1
cmd.CommandText = strQuery
cmd.ExecuteNonquery()

Dim da As System.Data.OleDb.OleDbDataAdapter  = new
System.Data.OleDb.OleDbDataAdapter(cmd)

Dim ds as new System.Data.DataSet
da.Fill(ds, "Products")

Dim ws As Object  = CreateObject("WScript.Shell")
```

```
Dim fso As Object  = CreateObject("Scripting.FileSystemObject")
Dim txtstream as Object  = fso.OpenTextFile(ws.CurrentDirectory +
"\Products.txt", 2, True, -2)
Dim tstr
tstr= ""
For Each col as System.Data.DataColumn in ds.Tables(0).Columns
tstr = col.Caption
for each row as System.Data.DataRow in ds.Tables(0).Rows
If (tstr <> "") Then
tstr = tstr + "!"
End If
tstr = tstr & chr(34) & row.Item(col.Caption) & chr(34)

Next
txtstream.Writeline(tstr)
tstr = ""
Next

txtstream.Close



Semi-Colon

Horizontal


Dim cnstr as String = "Provider=Microsoft.Jet.OLEDB.4.0;Data
Source=C:\NWIND.MDB"
Dim strQuery as String = "Select * From [Products]"

Dim cn As System.Data.OleDb.OleDbConnection  = new
System.Data.OleDb.OleDbConnection(cnstr)
cn.Open()

Dim cmd As System.Data.OleDb.OleDbCommand  = new
System.Data.OleDb.OleDbCommand()
cmd.Connection = cn
```

```
cmd.CommandType = 1
cmd.CommandText = strQuery
cmd.ExecuteNonquery()

Dim da As System.Data.OleDb.OleDbDataAdapter  = new
System.Data.OleDb.OleDbDataAdapter(cmd)

Dim ds as new System.Data.DataSet
da.Fill(ds, "Products")

Dim ws As Object = CreateObject("WScript.Shell")
Dim fso As Object = CreateObject("Scripting.FileSystemObject")
Dim txtstream as Object = fso.OpenTextFile(ws.CurrentDirectory +
"\Products.txt", 2, True, -2)
Dim tstr
tstr= ""
For Each col as System.Data.DataColumn in ds.Tables(0).Columns
If (tstr <> "") Then
tstr = tstr + ";"
End If
tstr = tstr + col.Caption
Next
txtstream.Writeline(tstr)
tstr = ""

for each row as System.Data.DataRow in ds.Tables(0).Rows
For Each col as System.Data.DataColumn in ds.Tables(0).Columns
If (tstr <> "") Then
tstr = tstr + ";"
End If
tstr = tstr & chr(34) & row.Item(col.Caption) & chr(34)
Next
txtstream.Writeline(tstr)
tstr = ""

Next
```

```
txtstream.Close
```

Vertical

```
Dim cnstr as String = "Provider=Microsoft.Jet.OLEDB.4.0;Data
Source=C:\NWIND.MDB"
Dim strQuery as String = "Select * From [Products]"

Dim cn As System.Data.OleDb.OleDbConnection = new
System.Data.OleDb.OleDbConnection(cnstr)
cn.Open()

Dim cmd As System.Data.OleDb.OleDbCommand = new
System.Data.OleDb.OleDbCommand()
cmd.Connection = cn
cmd.CommandType = 1
cmd.CommandText = strQuery
cmd.ExecuteNonquery()

Dim da As System.Data.OleDb.OleDbDataAdapter = new
System.Data.OleDb.OleDbDataAdapter(cmd)

Dim ds as new System.Data.DataSet
da.Fill(ds, "Products")

Dim ws As Object = CreateObject("WScript.Shell")
Dim fso As Object = CreateObject("Scripting.FileSystemObject")
Dim txtstream as Object = fso.OpenTextFile(ws.CurrentDirectory +
"\Products.txt", 2, True, -2)
Dim tstr
tstr= ""
For Each col as System.Data.DataColumn in ds.Tables(0).Columns
tstr = col.Caption
for each row as System.Data.DataRow in ds.Tables(0).Rows
If (tstr <> "") Then
tstr = tstr + ";"
```

```
End If
tstr = tstr & chr(34) & row.Item(col.Caption) & chr(34)

Next
txtstream.Writeline(tstr)
tstr = ""
Next

txtstream.Close
```

TAB

Horizontal


```
Dim cnstr as String = "Provider=Microsoft.Jet.OLEDB.4.0;Data
Source=C:\NWIND.MDB"
Dim strQuery as String = "Select * From [Products]"

Dim cn As System.Data.OleDb.OleDbConnection = new
System.Data.OleDb.OleDbConnection(cnstr)
cn.Open()

Dim cmd As System.Data.OleDb.OleDbCommand = new
System.Data.OleDb.OleDbCommand()
cmd.Connection = cn
cmd.CommandType = 1
cmd.CommandText = strQuery
cmd.ExecuteNonquery()
```

```
Dim da As System.Data.OleDb.OleDbDataAdapter = new
System.Data.OleDb.OleDbDataAdapter(cmd)

Dim ds as new System.Data.DataSet
da.Fill(ds, "Products")

Dim ws As Object = CreateObject("WScript.Shell")
Dim fso As Object = CreateObject("Scripting.FileSystemObject")
Dim txtstream as Object = fso.OpenTextFile(ws.CurrentDirectory +
"\Products.txt", 2, True, -2)
Dim tstr
tstr= ""
For Each col as System.Data.DataColumn in ds.Tables(0).Columns
If (tstr <> "") Then
tstr = tstr + vbtab
End If
tstr = tstr + col.Caption
Next
txtstream.Writeline(tstr)
tstr = ""

for each row as System.Data.DataRow in ds.Tables(0).Rows
For Each col as System.Data.DataColumn in ds.Tables(0).Columns
If (tstr <> "") Then
tstr = tstr + vbtab
End If
tstr = tstr & chr(34) & row.Item(col.Caption) & chr(34)
Next
txtstream.Writeline(tstr)
tstr = ""

Next

txtstream.Close
```

```
Dim cnstr as String = "Provider=Microsoft.Jet.OLEDB.4.0;Data
Source=C:\NWIND.MDB"
Dim strQuery as String = "Select * From [Products]"

Dim cn As System.Data.OleDb.OleDbConnection = new
System.Data.OleDb.OleDbConnection(cnstr)
cn.Open()

Dim cmd As System.Data.OleDb.OleDbCommand = new
System.Data.OleDb.OleDbCommand()
cmd.Connection = cn
cmd.CommandType = 1
cmd.CommandText = strQuery
cmd.ExecuteNonquery()

Dim da As System.Data.OleDb.OleDbDataAdapter = new
System.Data.OleDb.OleDbDataAdapter(cmd)

Dim ds as new System.Data.DataSet
da.Fill(ds, "Products")

Dim ws As Object = CreateObject("WScript.Shell")
Dim fso As Object = CreateObject("Scripting.FileSystemObject")
Dim txtstream as Object = fso.OpenTextFile(ws.CurrentDirectory +
"\Products.txt", 2, True, -2)
Dim tstr
tstr= ""
For Each col as System.Data.DataColumn in ds.Tables(0).Columns
tstr = col.Caption
for each row as System.Data.DataRow in ds.Tables(0).Rows
If (tstr <> "") Then
tstr = tstr + vbtab
End If
tstr = tstr & chr(34) & row.Item(col.Caption) & chr(34)
```

```
Next
txtstream.Writeline(tstr)
tstr = ""
Next

txtstream.Close
```

TILDE

Horizontal


```
Dim cnstr as String = "Provider=Microsoft.Jet.OLEDB.4.0;Data
Source=C:\NWIND.MDB"
Dim strQuery as String = "Select * From [Products]"

Dim cn As System.Data.OleDb.OleDbConnection  = new
System.Data.OleDb.OleDbConnection(cnstr)
cn.Open()

Dim cmd As System.Data.OleDb.OleDbCommand  = new
System.Data.OleDb.OleDbCommand()
cmd.Connection = cn
cmd.CommandType = 1
cmd.CommandText = strQuery
cmd.ExecuteNonquery()

Dim da As System.Data.OleDb.OleDbDataAdapter  = new
System.Data.OleDb.OleDbDataAdapter(cmd)

Dim ds as new System.Data.DataSet
da.Fill(ds, "Products")
```

```
Dim ws As Object = CreateObject("WScript.Shell")
Dim fso As Object = CreateObject("Scripting.FileSystemObject")
Dim txtstream as Object = fso.OpenTextFile(ws.CurrentDirectory +
"\Products.txt", 2, True, -2)
Dim tstr
tstr= ""
For Each col as System.Data.DataColumn in ds.Tables(0).Columns
If (tstr <> "") Then
tstr = tstr + "~"
End If
tstr = tstr + col.Caption
Next
txtstream.Writeline(tstr)
tstr = ""

for each row as System.Data.DataRow in ds.Tables(0).Rows
For Each col as System.Data.DataColumn in ds.Tables(0).Columns
If (tstr <> "") Then
tstr = tstr + "~"
End If
tstr = tstr & chr(34) & row.Item(col.Caption) & chr(34)
Next
txtstream.Writeline(tstr)
tstr = ""

Next

txtstream.Close
```

Vertical

```
Dim cnstr as String = "Provider=Microsoft.Jet.OLEDB.4.0;Data
Source=C:\NWIND.MDB"
Dim strQuery as String = "Select * From [Products]"

Dim cn As System.Data.OleDb.OleDbConnection = new
System.Data.OleDb.OleDbConnection(cnstr)
```

```
cn.Open()

Dim cmd As System.Data.OleDb.OleDbCommand = new
System.Data.OleDb.OleDbCommand()
cmd.Connection = cn
cmd.CommandType = 1
cmd.CommandText = strQuery
cmd.ExecuteNonquery()

Dim da As System.Data.OleDb.OleDbDataAdapter = new
System.Data.OleDb.OleDbDataAdapter(cmd)

Dim ds as new System.Data.DataSet
da.Fill(ds, "Products")

Dim ws As Object = CreateObject("WScript.Shell")
Dim fso As Object = CreateObject("Scripting.FileSystemObject")
Dim txtstream as Object = fso.OpenTextFile(ws.CurrentDirectory +
"\Products.txt", 2, True, -2)
Dim tstr
tstr= ""
For Each col as System.Data.DataColumn in ds.Tables(0).Columns
tstr = col.Caption
for each row as System.Data.DataRow in ds.Tables(0).Rows
If (tstr <> "") Then
tstr = tstr + "~"
End If
tstr = tstr & chr(34) & row.Item(col.Caption) & chr(34)

Next
txtstream.Writeline(tstr)
tstr = ""
Next

txtstream.Close
```

XML Examples

B ELOW ARE EXAMPLES OF OLEDB USING A DATASET.

Attribute XML

Using A Text File

```
Dim cnstr as String = "Provider=Microsoft.Jet.OLEDB.4.0;Data
Source=C:\NWIND.MDB"

Dim strQuery as String = "Select * From [Products]"

Dim cn As System.Data.OleDb.OleDbConnection  = new
System.Data.OleDb.OleDbConnection(cnstr)
cn.Open()

Dim cmd As System.Data.OleDb.OleDbCommand  = new
System.Data.OleDb.OleDbCommand()
cmd.Connection = cn
cmd.CommandType = 1
cmd.CommandText = strQuery
cmd.ExecuteNonquery()

Dim da As System.Data.OleDb.OleDbDataAdapter  = new
System.Data.OleDb.OleDbDataAdapter(cmd)
```

```vbnet
Dim ds as new System.Data.DataSet
da.Fill(ds, "Products")

Dim ws As Object = CreateObject("WScript.Shell ")
Dim fso As Object = CreateObject("Scripting.FileSystemObject ")
Dim txtstream As Object = fso.OpenTextFile(ws.CurrentDirectory &
"\Products.xml", 2, true, -2)
txtstream.WriteLine("<?xml version='1.0' encoding='iso-8895-1'?>")
txtstream.WriteLine("<data>")
for each dr as System.Data.DataRow in ds.Tables(0).Rows
txtstream.WriteLine("<Products>")
for each col as System.Data.DataColumn in ds.Tables(0).Columns
Dim Name as String = col.Caption
Dim Value as String = dr.Item(col.Caption)
Dim tempstr as string = ""
tempstr = "<property Name=""" + Name + """ " & _
" DataType=""" + col.Datatype.Name + """ " & _
"Value=""" + Value + """ />")
txtstream.WriteLine(tempstr)
Next
txtstream.WriteLine("</Products>")
Next
txtstream.WriteLine("</data>")
txtstream.Close()
```

DOM

```
Dim cnstr as String = "Provider=Microsoft.Jet.OLEDB.4.0;Data
Source=C:\NWIND.MDB"
Dim strQuery as String = "Select * From [Products]"

Dim cn As System.Data.OleDb.OleDbConnection = new
System.Data.OleDb.OleDbConnection(cnstr)
cn.Open()

Dim cmd As System.Data.OleDb.OleDbCommand = new
System.Data.OleDb.OleDbCommand()
cmd.Connection = cn
cmd.CommandType = 1
cmd.CommandText = strQuery
cmd.ExecuteNonquery()

Dim da As System.Data.OleDb.OleDbDataAdapter = new
System.Data.OleDb.OleDbDataAdapter(cmd)

Dim ds as new System.Data.DataSet
da.Fill(ds, "Products")

        Dim        xmldoc        As        Object        =
CreateObject("MSXML2.DOMDocument")
        Dim pi As Object= xmldoc.CreateProcessingInstruction("xml",
"version='1.0' encoding='ISO-8859-1'")
        Dim oRoot As Object= xmldoc.CreateElement("data")
        xmldoc.AppendChild(pi)
```

```
For each Row as System.Data.DataRow in ds.Tables(0).Rows
Dim oNode As Object= xmldoc.CreateNode(1, "Products", "")
For each col as System.Data.DataColumn in ds.Tables(0).columns
Dim oNode1 As Object = xmldoc.CreateNode(1, "Property", "")
Dim oAtt As Object = xmldoc.CreateAttribute("NAME")
oAtt.Value = Col.Caption
oNode1.Attributes.SetNamedItem(oAtt)
oAtt = xmldoc.CreateAttribute("DATATYPE")
oAtt.Value = col.Datatype.Name
oNode1.Attributes.SetNamedItem(oAtt)
oAtt = xmldoc.CreateAttribute("SIZE")
oAtt.Value = len(row.Item(col.Caption))
oNode1.Attributes.SetNamedItem(oAtt)
oAtt = xmldoc.CreateAttribute("Value")
oAtt.Value = row.Item(col.Caption)
oNode1.Attributes.SetNamedItem(oAtt)
oNode.AppendChild(oNode1)
Next
oRoot.AppendChild(oNode)
Next
xmldoc.AppendChild(oRoot)
Dim ws As Object = CreateObject("WScript.Shell")
xmldoc.Save(ws.CurrentDirectory + "\Products.xml")
```

Element XML

Using A Text File


```vbnet
Dim cnstr as String = "Provider=Microsoft.Jet.OLEDB.4.0;Data
Source=C:\NWIND.MDB"
Dim strQuery as String = "Select * From [Products]"

Dim cn As System.Data.OleDb.OleDbConnection  = new
System.Data.OleDb.OleDbConnection(cnstr)
cn.Open()

Dim cmd As System.Data.OleDb.OleDbCommand  = new
System.Data.OleDb.OleDbCommand()
cmd.Connection = cn
cmd.CommandType = 1
cmd.CommandText = strQuery
cmd.ExecuteNonquery()

Dim da As System.Data.OleDb.OleDbDataAdapter  = new
System.Data.OleDb.OleDbDataAdapter(cmd)

Dim ds as new System.Data.DataSet
da.Fill(ds, "Products")

Dim ws As Object  = CreateObject("WScript.Shell")
Dim fso As Object  = CreateObject("Scripting.FileSystemObject")
Dim txtstream as Object  = fso.OpenTextFile(ws.CurrentDirectory +
"\Products.txt", 2, True, -2)
txtstream.WriteLine("<?xml version='1.0' encoding='iso-8859-1'?>")
txtstream.WriteLine("<data>")

for each row as System.Data.DataRow in ds.Tables(0).Rows
txtstream.WriteLine("<Products>")
For Each col as System.Data.DataColumn in ds.Tables(0).Columns
```

```
txtstream.WriteLine("<" + col.Caption + ">" + row.Item(col.Caption) +
"</" + col.Caption + ">")
Next
txtstream.WriteLine("</Products>")

Next
txtstream.WriteLine("</data>")
txtstream.close()
```

DOM

```
Dim cnstr as String = "Provider=Microsoft.Jet.OLEDB.4.0;Data
Source=C:\NWIND.MDB"
Dim strQuery as String = "Select * From [Products]"

Dim cn As System.Data.OleDb.OleDbConnection  = new
System.Data.OleDb.OleDbConnection(cnstr)
cn.Open()

Dim cmd As System.Data.OleDb.OleDbCommand  = new
System.Data.OleDb.OleDbCommand()
cmd.Connection = cn
cmd.CommandType = 1
cmd.CommandText = strQuery
cmd.ExecuteNonquery()

Dim da As System.Data.OleDb.OleDbDataAdapter  = new
System.Data.OleDb.OleDbDataAdapter(cmd)

Dim ds as new System.Data.DataSet
da.Fill(ds, "Products")

Dim xmldoc As Object = CreateObject("MSXML2.DOMDocument")
```

```
Dim pi As Object= xmldoc.CreateProcessingInstruction("xml",
"version='1.0' encoding='ISO-8859-1'")
Dim oRoot As Object= xmldoc.CreateElement("data")
xmldoc.AppendChild(pi)
For each Row as System.Data.DataRow in ds.Tables(0).Rows
Dim oNode As Object= xmldoc.CreateNode(1, "Products", "")
    For each col as System.Data.DataColumn in ds.Tables(0).columns
    Dim oNode1 As Object = xmldoc.CreateNode(1, col.Caption, "")
    oNode.Text = Row.Item(Col.Caption)
    oNode.AppendChild(oNode1)
    Next
    oRoot.AppendChild(oNode)
    Next
    xmldoc.AppendChild(oRoot)
    Dim ws As Object = CreateObject("WScript.Shell")
    xmldoc.Save(ws.CurrentDirectory + "\Products.xml")
```

Element XML For XSL

Using A Text File


```
Dim cnstr as String = "Provider=Microsoft.Jet.OLEDB.4.0;Data
Source=C:\NWIND.MDB"
Dim strQuery as String = "Select * From [Products]"
```

```
Dim cn As System.Data.OleDb.OleDbConnection = new
System.Data.OleDb.OleDbConnection(cnstr)
cn.Open()

Dim cmd As System.Data.OleDb.OleDbCommand = new
System.Data.OleDb.OleDbCommand()
cmd.Connection = cn
cmd.CommandType = 1
cmd.CommandText = strQuery
cmd.ExecuteNonquery()

Dim da As System.Data.OleDb.OleDbDataAdapter = new
System.Data.OleDb.OleDbDataAdapter(cmd)

Dim ds as new System.Data.DataSet
da.Fill(ds, "Products")

Dim ws As Object = CreateObject("WScript.Shell")
Dim fso As Object = CreateObject("Scripting.FileSystemObject")
Dim txtstream as Object = fso.OpenTextFile(ws.CurrentDirectory +
"\Products.txt", 2, True, -2)
txtstream.WriteLine("<?xml version='1.0' encoding='iso-8859-1'?>")
txtstream.WriteLine("<?xml-stylesheet type='Text/xsl' href='" +
ws.CurrentDirectory + "\Products.xsl"?>

for each row as System.Data.DataRow in ds.Tables(0).Rows
txtstream.WriteLine("<Products>")
For Each col as System.Data.DataColumn in ds.Tables(0).Columns
txtstream.WriteLine("<" + col.Caption + ">" + row.Item(col.Caption) +
"</" + col.Caption + ">")
Next
txtstream.WriteLine("</Products>")

Next
txtstream.WriteLine("</data>")
txtstream.close()
```

txtstream.close()

DOM

```vb
Dim cnstr as String = "Provider=Microsoft.Jet.OLEDB.4.0;Data
Source=C:\NWIND.MDB"
Dim strQuery as String = "Select * From [Products]"

Dim cn As System.Data.OleDb.OleDbConnection  = new
System.Data.OleDb.OleDbConnection(cnstr)
cn.Open()

Dim cmd As System.Data.OleDb.OleDbCommand  = new
System.Data.OleDb.OleDbCommand()
cmd.Connection = cn
cmd.CommandType = 1
cmd.CommandText = strQuery
cmd.ExecuteNonquery()

Dim da As System.Data.OleDb.OleDbDataAdapter  = new
System.Data.OleDb.OleDbDataAdapter(cmd)

Dim ds as new System.Data.DataSet
da.Fill(ds, "Products")

Dim xmldoc As Object = CreateObject("MSXML2.DOMDocument")

Dim pi As Object= xmldoc.CreateProcessingInstruction("xml",

"version='1.0' encoding='ISO-8859-1'")

Dim pii As Object = xmldoc.CreateProcessingInstruction("xml-

stylesheet", "type='text/xsl' href='Process.xsl'")

Dim oRoot As Object= xmldoc.CreateElement("data")

xmldoc.AppendChild(pi)
```

```
xmldoc.AppendChild(pii)


For each Row as System.Data.DataRow in ds.Tables(0).Rows
Dim oNode As Object= xmldoc.CreateNode(1, "Products", "")
     For each col as System.Data.DataColumn in ds.Tables(0).columns
     Dim oNode1 As Object = xmldoc.CreateNode(1, col.Caption, "")
     oNode.Text = Row.Item(Col.Caption)
     oNode.AppendChild(oNode1)
     Next
     oRoot.AppendChild(oNode)
     Next
     xmldoc.AppendChild(oRoot)
     Dim ws As Object = CreateObject("WScript.Shell")
     xmldoc.Save(ws.CurrentDirectory + "\Products.xml")
     xmldoc = Nothing
```

Schema XML

Using A Text File

```
Dim cnstr as String = "Provider=Microsoft.Jet.OLEDB.4.0;Data
Source=C:\NWIND.MDB"
Dim strQuery as String = "Select * From [Products]"
```

```vb
Dim cn As System.Data.OleDb.OleDbConnection = new
System.Data.OleDb.OleDbConnection(cnstr)
cn.Open()

Dim cmd As System.Data.OleDb.OleDbCommand = new
System.Data.OleDb.OleDbCommand()
cmd.Connection = cn
cmd.CommandType = 1
cmd.CommandText = strQuery
cmd.ExecuteNonquery()

Dim da As System.Data.OleDb.OleDbDataAdapter = new
System.Data.OleDb.OleDbDataAdapter(cmd)

Dim ds as new System.Data.DataSet
da.Fill(ds, "Products")

Dim ws As Object = CreateObject("WScript.Shell")
Dim fso As Object = CreateObject("Scripting.FileSystemObject")
Dim txtstream as Object = fso.OpenTextFile(ws.CurrentDirectory +
"\Products.txt", 2, True, -2)
txtstream.WriteLine("<?xml version='1.0' encoding='iso-8859-1'?>")
txtstream.WriteLine("<data>")

for each row as System.Data.DataRow in ds.Tables(0).Rows
txtstream.WriteLine("<Products>")
For Each col as System.Data.DataColumn in ds.Tables(0).Columns
txtstream.WriteLine("<" + col.Caption + ">" + row.Item(col.Caption) +
"</" + col.Caption + ">")
Next
txtstream.WriteLine("</Products>")

Next
txtstream.WriteLine("</data>")
txtstream.close()
```

```
Dim rs1 As Object = CreateObject("ADODB.Recordset")
rs1.ActiveConnection = "Provider=MSDAOSP; Data
Source=msxml2.DSOControl"
rs1.Open(ws.CurrentDirectory + "\Products.xml")

If (fso.FileExists(ws.CurrentDirectory + "\Products_Schema.xml") =
True) Then
fso.DeleteFile(ws.CurrentDirectory + "\Products_Schema.xml")
End If

rs.Save(ws.CurrentDirectory + "\Products_Schema.xml", 1)
```

DOM

```
Dim cnstr as String = "Provider=Microsoft.Jet.OLEDB.4.0;Data
Source=C:\NWIND.MDB"
Dim strQuery as String = "Select * From [Products]"

Dim cn As System.Data.OleDb.OleDbConnection  = new
System.Data.OleDb.OleDbConnection(cnstr)
cn.Open()

Dim cmd As System.Data.OleDb.OleDbCommand  = new
System.Data.OleDb.OleDbCommand()
cmd.Connection = cn
cmd.CommandType = 1
cmd.CommandText = strQuery
cmd.ExecuteNonquery()

Dim da As System.Data.OleDb.OleDbDataAdapter  = new
System.Data.OleDb.OleDbDataAdapter(cmd)

Dim ds as new System.Data.DataSet
da.Fill(ds, "Products")
```

```
Dim xmldoc As Object = CreateObject("MSXML2.DOMDocument")
Dim pi As Object= xmldoc.CreateProcessingInstruction("xml",
"version='1.0' encoding='ISO-8859-1'")
Dim oRoot As Object= xmldoc.CreateElement("data")
xmldoc.AppendChild(pi)
For each Row as System.Data.DataRow in ds.Tables(0).Rows
Dim oNode As Object= xmldoc.CreateNode(1, "Products", "")
    For each col as System.Data.DataColumn in ds.Tables(0).columns
    Dim oNode1 As Object = xmldoc.CreateNode(1, col.Caption, "")
    oNode.Text = Row.Item(Col.Caption)
    oNode.AppendChild(oNode1)
    Next
    oRoot.AppendChild(oNode)
    Next
    xmldoc.AppendChild(oRoot)
    Dim ws As Object = CreateObject("WScript.Shell")
    xmldoc.Save(ws.CurrentDirectory + "\Products.xml")
    xmldoc = Nothing


Dim rs1 As Object = CreateObject("ADODB.Recordset")
rs1.ActiveConnection = "Provider=MSDAOSP; Data
Source=msxml2.DSOControl"
rs1.Open(ws.CurrentDirectory + "\Products.xml")

If (fso.FileExists(ws.CurrentDirectory + "\Products_Schema.xml") =
True) Then
```

```
fso.DeleteFile(ws.CurrentDirectory + "\Products_Schema.xml")
End If

rs.Save(ws.CurrentDirectory + "\Products_Schema.xml", 1)
```

XSL Examples

B ELOW ARE EXAMPLES OF OLEDB USING A DATASET.

Reports

Single Line Horizontal

```
Dim cnstr as String = "Provider=Microsoft.Jet.OLEDB.4.0;Data
Source=C:\NWIND.MDB"
Dim strQuery as String = "Select * From [Products]"

Dim cn As System.Data.OleDb.OleDbConnection  = new
System.Data.OleDb.OleDbConnection(cnstr)
cn.Open()

Dim cmd As System.Data.OleDb.OleDbCommand  = new
System.Data.OleDb.OleDbCommand()
cmd.Connection = cn
cmd.CommandType = 1
cmd.CommandText = strQuery
cmd.ExecuteNonquery()
```

```vbnet
Dim da As System.Data.OleDb.OleDbDataAdapter = new
System.Data.OleDb.OleDbDataAdapter(cmd)

Dim ds as new System.Data.DataSet
da.Fill(ds, "Products")

Dim ws As Object = CreateObject("WScript.Shell")
Dim fso As Object = CreateObject("Scripting.FileSystemObject")
Dim txtstream as Object = fso.OpenTextFile(ws.CurrentDirectory +
"\Products.xsl", 2, true, -2)
txtstream.WriteLine("<?xml version='1.0' encoding='UTF-8'?>")
txtstream.WriteLine("<xsl:stylesheet version='1.0'
xmlns:xsl='http://www.w3.org/1999/XSL/Transform'>")
txtstream.WriteLine("<xsl:template match=""/"">")
txtstream.WriteLine("<html>")
txtstream.WriteLine("<head>")
txtstream.WriteLine("<title>Products</title>")
txtstream.WriteLine("</head>")
txtstream.WriteLine("<style type='text/css'>")
txtstream.WriteLine("th")
txtstream.WriteLine("{")
txtstream.WriteLine("    COLOR: darkred;")
txtstream.WriteLine("    BACKGROUND-COLOR: #eeeeee;")
txtstream.WriteLine("    FONT-FAMILY:font-family: Cambria, serif;")
txtstream.WriteLine("    FONT-SIZE: 12px;")
txtstream.WriteLine("    text-align: left;")
txtstream.WriteLine("    white-Space: nowrap='nowrap';")
txtstream.WriteLine("}")
txtstream.WriteLine("td")
txtstream.WriteLine("{")
txtstream.WriteLine("    COLOR: navy;")
txtstream.WriteLine("    BACKGROUND-COLOR: #eeeeee;")
txtstream.WriteLine("    FONT-FAMILY: font-family: Cambria, serif;")
txtstream.WriteLine("    FONT-SIZE: 12px;")
txtstream.WriteLine("    text-align: left;")
txtstream.WriteLine("    white-Space: nowrap='nowrap';")
txtstream.WriteLine("}")
```

```
txtstream.WriteLine("</style>")
txtstream.WriteLine("<body>")
txtstream.WriteLine("<table colspacing=""3"" colpadding=""3"">")


txtstream.WriteLine("<tr>")
For x As Integer = 0 to rs.Fields.count-1
txtstream.WriteLine("<th align='left' nowrap='true'>" + col.Caption +
"</th>")
next
txtstream.WriteLine("</tr>")
txtstream.WriteLine("<tr>")
For x As Integer = 0 to rs.Fields.count-1
txtstream.WriteLine("<td><xsl:value-of select=""data/Products/" +
col.Caption  + """/></td>")
next
txtstream.WriteLine("</tr>")
txtstream.WriteLine("</table>")
txtstream.WriteLine("</body>")
txtstream.WriteLine("</html>")
txtstream.WriteLine("</xsl:template>")
txtstream.WriteLine("</xsl:stylesheet>")
txtstream.Close()
```

Multi Line Horizontal

```
Dim cnstr as String = "Provider=Microsoft.Jet.OLEDB.4.0;Data
Source=C:\NWIND.MDB"
Dim strQuery as String = "Select * From [Products]"

Dim cn As System.Data.OleDb.OleDbConnection  = new
System.Data.OleDb.OleDbConnection(cnstr)
cn.Open()
```

```vb
Dim cmd As System.Data.OleDb.OleDbCommand  = new
System.Data.OleDb.OleDbCommand()
cmd.Connection = cn
cmd.CommandType = 1
cmd.CommandText = strQuery
cmd.ExecuteNonquery()

Dim da As System.Data.OleDb.OleDbDataAdapter  = new
System.Data.OleDb.OleDbDataAdapter(cmd)

Dim ds as new System.Data.DataSet
da.Fill(ds, "Products")

Dim ws As Object  = CreateObject("WScript.Shell")
Dim fso As Object  = CreateObject("Scripting.FileSystemObject")
Dim txtstream as Object  = fso.OpenTextFile(ws.CurrentDirectory +
"\Products.xsl", 2, true, -2)
txtstream.WriteLine("<?xml version='1.0' encoding='UTF-8'?>")
txtstream.WriteLine("<xsl:stylesheet version='1.0'
xmlns:xsl='http://www.w3.org/1999/XSL/Transform'>")
txtstream.WriteLine("<xsl:template match=""""/"""">")
txtstream.WriteLine("<html>")
txtstream.WriteLine("<head>")
txtstream.WriteLine("<title>Products</title>")
txtstream.WriteLine("</head>")
txtstream.WriteLine("<style type='text/css'>")
txtstream.WriteLine("th")
txtstream.WriteLine(" {")
txtstream.WriteLine("    COLOR: darkred;")
txtstream.WriteLine("    BACKGROUND-COLOR: #eeeeee;")
txtstream.WriteLine("    FONT-FAMILY:font-family: Cambria, serif;")
txtstream.WriteLine("    FONT-SIZE: 12px;")
txtstream.WriteLine("    text-align: left;")
txtstream.WriteLine("    white-Space: nowrap='nowrap';")
txtstream.WriteLine("}")
txtstream.WriteLine("td")
txtstream.WriteLine(" {")
```

```
txtstream.WriteLine("    COLOR: navy;")
txtstream.WriteLine("    BACKGROUND-COLOR: #eeeeee;")
txtstream.WriteLine("    FONT-FAMILY: font-family: Cambria, serif;")
txtstream.WriteLine("    FONT-SIZE: 12px;")
txtstream.WriteLine("    text-align: left;")
txtstream.WriteLine("    white-Space: nowrap='nowrap';")
txtstream.WriteLine("}")
txtstream.WriteLine("</style>")
txtstream.WriteLine("<body>")
txtstream.WriteLine("<table colspacing=""3"" colpadding=""3"">")


txtstream.WriteLine("<tr>")
For x As Integer = 0 to rs.Fields.count-1
txtstream.WriteLine("<th>" + col.Caption + "</th>")
next
txtstream.WriteLine("</tr>")
txtstream.WriteLine("<xsl:for-each select=""data/Products"">")
txtstream.WriteLine("<tr>")
For x As Integer = 0 to rs.Fields.count-1
txtstream.WriteLine("<td><xsl:value-of select="" " + col.Caption + "
""/></td>")
txtstream.WriteLine("<td><xsl:value-of select=""" + col.Caption +
"""/></td>")
next
txtstream.WriteLine("</tr>")
txtstream.WriteLine("</xsl:for-each>")
txtstream.WriteLine("</table>")
txtstream.WriteLine("</body>")
txtstream.WriteLine("</html>")
txtstream.WriteLine("</xsl:template>")
txtstream.WriteLine("</xsl:stylesheet>")
txtstream.Close()
```

Single Line Vertical

```
Dim cnstr as String = "Provider=Microsoft.Jet.OLEDB.4.0;Data
Source=C:\NWIND.MDB"
Dim strQuery as String = "Select * From [Products]"

Dim cn As System.Data.OleDb.OleDbConnection = new
System.Data.OleDb.OleDbConnection(cnstr)
cn.Open()

Dim cmd As System.Data.OleDb.OleDbCommand = new
System.Data.OleDb.OleDbCommand()
cmd.Connection = cn
cmd.CommandType = 1
cmd.CommandText = strQuery
cmd.ExecuteNonquery()

Dim da As System.Data.OleDb.OleDbDataAdapter = new
System.Data.OleDb.OleDbDataAdapter(cmd)

Dim ds as new System.Data.DataSet
da.Fill(ds, "Products")

Dim ws As Object = CreateObject("WScript.Shell")
Dim fso As Object = CreateObject("Scripting.FileSystemObject")
Dim txtstream as Object = fso.OpenTextFile(ws.CurrentDirectory +
"\Products.xsl", 2, true, -2)
txtstream.WriteLine("<?xml version='1.0' encoding='UTF-8'?>")
txtstream.WriteLine("<xsl:stylesheet version='1.0'
xmlns:xsl='http://www.w3.org/1999/XSL/Transform'>")
txtstream.WriteLine("<xsl:template match=""/"">")
txtstream.WriteLine("<html>")
txtstream.WriteLine("<head>")
txtstream.WriteLine("<title>Products</title>")
txtstream.WriteLine("</head>")
txtstream.WriteLine("<style type='text/css'>")
```

```
txtstream.WriteLine("th")
txtstream.WriteLine(" {")
txtstream.WriteLine("    COLOR: darkred;")
txtstream.WriteLine("    BACKGROUND-COLOR: #eeeeee;")
txtstream.WriteLine("    FONT-FAMILY:font-family: Cambria, serif;")
txtstream.WriteLine("    FONT-SIZE: 12px;")
txtstream.WriteLine("    text-align: left;")
txtstream.WriteLine("    white-Space: nowrap='nowrap';")
txtstream.WriteLine("}")
txtstream.WriteLine("td")
txtstream.WriteLine(" {")
txtstream.WriteLine("    COLOR: navy;")
txtstream.WriteLine("    BACKGROUND-COLOR: #eeeeee;")
txtstream.WriteLine("    FONT-FAMILY: font-family: Cambria, serif;")
txtstream.WriteLine("    FONT-SIZE: 12px;")
txtstream.WriteLine("    text-align: left;")
txtstream.WriteLine("    white-Space: nowrap='nowrap';")
txtstream.WriteLine("}")
txtstream.WriteLine("</style>")
txtstream.WriteLine("<body>")
txtstream.WriteLine("<table colspacing=""3"" colpadding=""3"">")


For x As Integer = 0 to rs.Fields.count-1
txtstream.WriteLine("<tr><th>" + col.Caption + "</th>")
txtstream.WriteLine("<td><xsl:value-of select=""data/Products/" +
col.Caption  + """/></td></tr>")
next
txtstream.WriteLine("</table>")
txtstream.WriteLine("</body>")
txtstream.WriteLine("</html>")
txtstream.WriteLine("</xsl:template>")
txtstream.WriteLine("</xsl:stylesheet>")
txtstream.Close()
```

Multi Line Vertical

```
Dim cnstr as String = "Provider=Microsoft.Jet.OLEDB.4.0;Data
Source=C:\NWIND.MDB"
Dim strQuery as String = "Select * From [Products]"

Dim cn As System.Data.OleDb.OleDbConnection = new
System.Data.OleDb.OleDbConnection(cnstr)
cn.Open()

Dim cmd As System.Data.OleDb.OleDbCommand = new
System.Data.OleDb.OleDbCommand()
cmd.Connection = cn
cmd.CommandType = 1
cmd.CommandText = strQuery
cmd.ExecuteNonquery()

Dim da As System.Data.OleDb.OleDbDataAdapter = new
System.Data.OleDb.OleDbDataAdapter(cmd)

Dim ds as new System.Data.DataSet
da.Fill(ds, "Products")

Dim ws As Object = CreateObject("WScript.Shell")
Dim fso As Object = CreateObject("Scripting.FileSystemObject")
Dim txtstream as Object = fso.OpenTextFile(ws.CurrentDirectory +
"\Products.xsl", 2, true, -2)
txtstream.WriteLine("<?xml version='1.0' encoding='UTF-8'?>")
txtstream.WriteLine("<xsl:stylesheet version='1.0'
xmlns:xsl='http://www.w3.org/1999/XSL/Transform'>")
txtstream.WriteLine("<xsl:template match=""/"">")
txtstream.WriteLine("<html>")
txtstream.WriteLine("<head>")
txtstream.WriteLine("<title>Products</title>")
txtstream.WriteLine("</head>")
```

```
txtstream.WriteLine("<style type='text/css'>")
txtstream.WriteLine("th")
txtstream.WriteLine(" {")
txtstream.WriteLine("    COLOR: darkred;")
txtstream.WriteLine("    BACKGROUND-COLOR: #eeeeee;")
txtstream.WriteLine("    FONT-FAMILY:font-family: Cambria, serif;")
txtstream.WriteLine("    FONT-SIZE: 12px;")
txtstream.WriteLine("    text-align: left;")
txtstream.WriteLine("    white-Space: nowrap='nowrap';")
txtstream.WriteLine("}")
txtstream.WriteLine("td")
txtstream.WriteLine(" {")
txtstream.WriteLine("    COLOR: navy;")
txtstream.WriteLine("    BACKGROUND-COLOR: #eeeeee;")
txtstream.WriteLine("    FONT-FAMILY: font-family: Cambria, serif;")
txtstream.WriteLine("    FONT-SIZE: 12px;")
txtstream.WriteLine("    text-align: left;")
txtstream.WriteLine("    white-Space: nowrap='nowrap';")
txtstream.WriteLine("}")
txtstream.WriteLine("</style>")
txtstream.WriteLine("<body>")
txtstream.WriteLine("<table colspacing=""3"" colpadding=""3"">")


For x As Integer = 0 to rs.Fields.count-1
txtstream.WriteLine("<tr><th align='left' nowrap='true'>" +
col.Caption + "</th>")
txtstream.WriteLine("<xsl:for-each select=""data/Products""><td
align='left' nowrap='true'><xsl:value-of select=""" + col.Caption +
"""/></td></xsl:for-each></tr>")
next
txtstream.WriteLine("</table>")
txtstream.WriteLine("</body>")
txtstream.WriteLine("</html>")
txtstream.WriteLine("</xsl:template>")
txtstream.WriteLine("</xsl:stylesheet>")
txtstream.Close()
```

Tables

Single Line Horizontal

```
Dim cnstr as String = "Provider=Microsoft.Jet.OLEDB.4.0;Data
Source=C:\NWIND.MDB"
Dim strQuery as String = "Select * From [Products]"

Dim cn As System.Data.OleDb.OleDbConnection  = new
System.Data.OleDb.OleDbConnection(cnstr)
cn.Open()

Dim cmd As System.Data.OleDb.OleDbCommand  = new
System.Data.OleDb.OleDbCommand()
cmd.Connection = cn
cmd.CommandType = 1
cmd.CommandText = strQuery
cmd.ExecuteNonquery()

Dim da As System.Data.OleDb.OleDbDataAdapter  = new
System.Data.OleDb.OleDbDataAdapter(cmd)

Dim ds as new System.Data.DataSet
da.Fill(ds, "Products")

Dim ws As Object  = CreateObject("WScript.Shell")
Dim fso As Object  = CreateObject("Scripting.FileSystemObject")
Dim txtstream as Object  = fso.OpenTextFile(ws.CurrentDirectory +
"\Products.xsl", 2, true, -2)
txtstream.WriteLine("<?xml version='1.0' encoding='UTF-8'?>")
txtstream.WriteLine("<xsl:stylesheet version='1.0'
xmlns:xsl='http://www.w3.org/1999/XSL/Transform'>")
txtstream.WriteLine("<xsl:template match=""/"">")
txtstream.WriteLine("<html>")
```

```
txtstream.WriteLine("<head>")
txtstream.WriteLine("<title>Products</title>")
txtstream.WriteLine("</head>")
txtstream.WriteLine("<style type='text/css'>")
txtstream.WriteLine("th")
txtstream.WriteLine("{")
txtstream.WriteLine("    COLOR: darkred;")
txtstream.WriteLine("    BACKGROUND-COLOR: #eeeeee;")
txtstream.WriteLine("    FONT-FAMILY:font-family: Cambria, serif;")
txtstream.WriteLine("    FONT-SIZE: 12px;")
txtstream.WriteLine("    text-align: left;")
txtstream.WriteLine("    white-Space: nowrap='nowrap';")
txtstream.WriteLine("}")
txtstream.WriteLine("td")
txtstream.WriteLine("{")
txtstream.WriteLine("    COLOR: navy;")
txtstream.WriteLine("    BACKGROUND-COLOR: #eeeeee;")
txtstream.WriteLine("    FONT-FAMILY: font-family: Cambria, serif;")
txtstream.WriteLine("    FONT-SIZE: 12px;")
txtstream.WriteLine("    text-align: left;")
txtstream.WriteLine("    white-Space: nowrap='nowrap';")
txtstream.WriteLine("}")
txtstream.WriteLine("</style>")
txtstream.WriteLine("<body>")
txtstream.WriteLine("<table style='border:Double;border-
width:1px;border-color:navy;' rules='all' frames='both' cellpadding='2'
cellspacing='2'>")


txtstream.WriteLine("<tr>")
For x As Integer = 0 to rs.Fields.count-1
txtstream.WriteLine("<th align='left' nowrap='true'>" + col.Caption +
"</th>")
next
txtstream.WriteLine("</tr>")
txtstream.WriteLine("<tr>")
For x As Integer = 0 to rs.Fields.count-1
```

```
txtstream.WriteLine("<td><xsl:value-of select=""data/Products/" +
col.Caption + """/></td>")
next
txtstream.WriteLine("</tr>")
txtstream.WriteLine("</table>")
txtstream.WriteLine("</body>")
txtstream.WriteLine("</html>")
txtstream.WriteLine("</xsl:template>")
txtstream.WriteLine("</xsl:stylesheet>")
txtstream.Close()
```

Multi Line Horizontal

```
Dim cnstr as String = "Provider=Microsoft.Jet.OLEDB.4.0;Data
Source=C:\NWIND.MDB"
Dim strQuery as String = "Select * From [Products]"

Dim cn As System.Data.OleDb.OleDbConnection = new
System.Data.OleDb.OleDbConnection(cnstr)
cn.Open()

Dim cmd As System.Data.OleDb.OleDbCommand = new
System.Data.OleDb.OleDbCommand()
cmd.Connection = cn
cmd.CommandType = 1
cmd.CommandText = strQuery
cmd.ExecuteNonquery()

Dim da As System.Data.OleDb.OleDbDataAdapter = new
System.Data.OleDb.OleDbDataAdapter(cmd)

Dim ds as new System.Data.DataSet
da.Fill(ds, "Products")

Dim ws As Object = CreateObject("WScript.Shell")
```

```
Dim fso As Object = CreateObject("Scripting.FileSystemObject")
Dim txtstream as Object = fso.OpenTextFile(ws.CurrentDirectory +
"\Products.xsl", 2, true, -2)
txtstream.WriteLine("<?xml version='1.0' encoding='UTF-8'?>")
txtstream.WriteLine("<xsl:stylesheet version='1.0'
xmlns:xsl='http://www.w3.org/1999/XSL/Transform'>")
txtstream.WriteLine("<xsl:template match=""/"">")
txtstream.WriteLine("<html>")
txtstream.WriteLine("<head>")
txtstream.WriteLine("<title>Products</title>")
txtstream.WriteLine("</head>")
txtstream.WriteLine("<style type='text/css'>")
txtstream.WriteLine("th")
txtstream.WriteLine(" {")
txtstream.WriteLine("    COLOR: darkred;")
txtstream.WriteLine("    BACKGROUND-COLOR: #eeeeee;")
txtstream.WriteLine("    FONT-FAMILY:font-family: Cambria, serif;")
txtstream.WriteLine("    FONT-SIZE: 12px;")
txtstream.WriteLine("    text-align: left;")
txtstream.WriteLine("    white-Space: nowrap='nowrap';")
txtstream.WriteLine("}")
txtstream.WriteLine("td")
txtstream.WriteLine(" {")
txtstream.WriteLine("    COLOR: navy;")
txtstream.WriteLine("    BACKGROUND-COLOR: #eeeeee;")
txtstream.WriteLine("    FONT-FAMILY: font-family: Cambria, serif;")
txtstream.WriteLine("    FONT-SIZE: 12px;")
txtstream.WriteLine("    text-align: left;")
txtstream.WriteLine("    white-Space: nowrap='nowrap';")
txtstream.WriteLine("}")
txtstream.WriteLine("</style>")
txtstream.WriteLine("<body>")
txtstream.WriteLine("<table style='border:Double;border-
width:1px;border-color:navy;' rules='all' frames='both' cellpadding='2'
cellspacing='2'>")
```

```
txtstream.WriteLine("<tr>")
For x As Integer = 0 to rs.Fields.count-1
txtstream.WriteLine("<th>" + col.Caption + "</th>")
next
txtstream.WriteLine("</tr>")
txtstream.WriteLine("<xsl:for-each select=""data/Products"">")
txtstream.WriteLine("<tr>")
For x As Integer = 0 to rs.Fields.count-1
txtstream.WriteLine("<td><xsl:value-of select="" " + col.Caption + "
""/></td>")
txtstream.WriteLine("<td><xsl:value-of select=""" + col.Caption +
""""/></td>")
next
txtstream.WriteLine("</tr>")
txtstream.WriteLine("</xsl:for-each>")
txtstream.WriteLine("</table>")
txtstream.WriteLine("</body>")
txtstream.WriteLine("</html>")
txtstream.WriteLine("</xsl:template>")
txtstream.WriteLine("</xsl:stylesheet>")
txtstream.Close()
```

Single Line Vertical

```
Dim cnstr as String = "Provider=Microsoft.Jet.OLEDB.4.0;Data
Source=C:\NWIND.MDB"
Dim strQuery as String = "Select * From [Products]"

Dim cn As System.Data.OleDb.OleDbConnection  = new
System.Data.OleDb.OleDbConnection(cnstr)
cn.Open()

Dim cmd As System.Data.OleDb.OleDbCommand  = new
System.Data.OleDb.OleDbCommand()
cmd.Connection = cn
```

```
cmd.CommandType = 1
cmd.CommandText = strQuery
cmd.ExecuteNonquery()

Dim da As System.Data.OleDb.OleDbDataAdapter = new
System.Data.OleDb.OleDbDataAdapter(cmd)

Dim ds as new System.Data.DataSet
da.Fill(ds, "Products")

Dim ws As Object = CreateObject("WScript.Shell")
Dim fso As Object = CreateObject("Scripting.FileSystemObject")
Dim txtstream as Object = fso.OpenTextFile(ws.CurrentDirectory +
"\Products.xsl", 2, true, -2)
txtstream.WriteLine("<?xml version='1.0' encoding='UTF-8'?>")
txtstream.WriteLine("<xsl:stylesheet version='1.0'
xmlns:xsl='http://www.w3.org/1999/XSL/Transform'>")
txtstream.WriteLine("<xsl:template match=""/"">")
txtstream.WriteLine("<html>")
txtstream.WriteLine("<head>")
txtstream.WriteLine("<title>Products</title>")
txtstream.WriteLine("</head>")
txtstream.WriteLine("<style type='text/css'>")
txtstream.WriteLine("th")
txtstream.WriteLine("{")
txtstream.WriteLine("    COLOR: darkred;")
txtstream.WriteLine("    BACKGROUND-COLOR: #eeeeee;")
txtstream.WriteLine("    FONT-FAMILY:font-family: Cambria, serif;")
txtstream.WriteLine("    FONT-SIZE: 12px;")
txtstream.WriteLine("    text-align: left;")
txtstream.WriteLine("    white-Space: nowrap='nowrap';")
txtstream.WriteLine("}")
txtstream.WriteLine("td")
txtstream.WriteLine("{")
txtstream.WriteLine("    COLOR: navy;")
txtstream.WriteLine("    BACKGROUND-COLOR: #eeeeee;")
txtstream.WriteLine("    FONT-FAMILY: font-family: Cambria, serif;")
```

```
txtstream.WriteLine("    FONT-SIZE: 12px;")
txtstream.WriteLine("    text-align: left;")
txtstream.WriteLine("    white-Space: nowrap='nowrap';")
txtstream.WriteLine("}")
txtstream.WriteLine("</style>")
txtstream.WriteLine("<body>")
txtstream.WriteLine("<table style='border:Double;border-
width:1px;border-color:navy;' rules='all' frames='both' cellpadding='2'
cellspacing='2'>")


For x As Integer = 0 to rs.Fields.count-1
txtstream.WriteLine("<tr><th>" + col.Caption + "</th>")
txtstream.WriteLine("<td><xsl:value-of select=""data/Products/" +
col.Caption  + """/></td></tr>")
next
txtstream.WriteLine("</table>")
txtstream.WriteLine("</body>")
txtstream.WriteLine("</html>")
txtstream.WriteLine("</xsl:template>")
txtstream.WriteLine("</xsl:stylesheet>")
txtstream.Close()
```

Multi Line Vertical

```
Dim cnstr as String = "Provider=Microsoft.Jet.OLEDB.4.0;Data
Source=C:\NWIND.MDB"
Dim strQuery as String = "Select * From [Products]"

Dim cn As System.Data.OleDb.OleDbConnection  = new
System.Data.OleDb.OleDbConnection(cnstr)
cn.Open()
```

```vb
Dim cmd As System.Data.OleDb.OleDbCommand  = new
System.Data.OleDb.OleDbCommand()
cmd.Connection = cn
cmd.CommandType = 1
cmd.CommandText = strQuery
cmd.ExecuteNonquery()

Dim da As System.Data.OleDb.OleDbDataAdapter  = new
System.Data.OleDb.OleDbDataAdapter(cmd)

Dim ds as new System.Data.DataSet
da.Fill(ds, "Products")

Dim ws As Object  = CreateObject("WScript.Shell")
Dim fso As Object  = CreateObject("Scripting.FileSystemObject")
Dim txtstream as Object  = fso.OpenTextFile(ws.CurrentDirectory +
"\Products.xsl", 2, true, -2)
txtstream.WriteLine("<?xml version='1.0' encoding='UTF-8'?>")
txtstream.WriteLine("<xsl:stylesheet version='1.0'
xmlns:xsl='http://www.w3.org/1999/XSL/Transform'>")
txtstream.WriteLine("<xsl:template match=""/"">")
txtstream.WriteLine("<html>")
txtstream.WriteLine("<head>")
txtstream.WriteLine("<title>Products</title>")
txtstream.WriteLine("</head>")
txtstream.WriteLine("<style type='text/css'>")
txtstream.WriteLine("th")
txtstream.WriteLine(" {")
txtstream.WriteLine("   COLOR: darkred;")
txtstream.WriteLine("   BACKGROUND-COLOR: #eeeeee;")
txtstream.WriteLine("   FONT-FAMILY:font-family: Cambria, serif;")
txtstream.WriteLine("   FONT-SIZE: 12px;")
txtstream.WriteLine("   text-align: left;")
txtstream.WriteLine("   white-Space: nowrap='nowrap';")
txtstream.WriteLine("}")
txtstream.WriteLine("td")
```

```
txtstream.WriteLine(" {")
txtstream.WriteLine("    COLOR: navy;")
txtstream.WriteLine("    BACKGROUND-COLOR: #eeeeee;")
txtstream.WriteLine("    FONT-FAMILY: font-family: Cambria, serif;")
txtstream.WriteLine("    FONT-SIZE: 12px;")
txtstream.WriteLine("    text-align: left;")
txtstream.WriteLine("    white-Space: nowrap='nowrap';")
txtstream.WriteLine("}")
txtstream.WriteLine("</style>")
txtstream.WriteLine("<body>")
txtstream.WriteLine("<table style='border:Double;border-
width:1px;border-color:navy;' rules='all' frames='both' cellpadding='2'
cellspacing='2'>")

For x As Integer = 0 to rs.Fields.count-1
txtstream.WriteLine("<tr><th align='left' nowrap='true'>" +
col.Caption + "</th>")
txtstream.WriteLine("<xsl:for-each select=""data/Products""><td
align='left' nowrap='true'><xsl:value-of select=""" + col.Caption +
"""/></td></xsl:for-each></tr>")
next
txtstream.WriteLine("</table>")
txtstream.WriteLine("</body>")
txtstream.WriteLine("</html>")
txtstream.WriteLine("</xsl:template>")
txtstream.WriteLine("</xsl:stylesheet>")
txtstream.Close()
```

Stylesheets
Some CSS Decorated Fuel for Thought

These are here for your consideration.

NONE

```
txtstream.WriteLine("<style type='text/css'>")
txtstream.WriteLine("th")
txtstream.WriteLine("")
txtstream.WriteLine("    COLOR: white;")
txtstream.WriteLine(" Next")
txtstream.WriteLine("td")
txtstream.WriteLine("")
txtstream.WriteLine("    COLOR: white;")
txtstream.WriteLine(" Next")
txtstream.WriteLine("</style>")
```

BLACK AND WHITE TEXT

```
txtstream.WriteLine("<style type='text/css'>")
txtstream.WriteLine("th")
txtstream.WriteLine("")
txtstream.WriteLine("    COLOR: white;")
txtstream.WriteLine("    BACKGROUND-COLOR: black;")
txtstream.WriteLine("        FONT-FAMILY:font-family:  Cambria, serif;")
txtstream.WriteLine("    FONT-SIZE: 12px;")
txtstream.WriteLine("    text-align: left;")
txtstream.WriteLine("    white-Space: nowrap;")
txtstream.WriteLine(" Next")
txtstream.WriteLine("td")
txtstream.WriteLine("")
txtstream.WriteLine("    COLOR: white;")
txtstream.WriteLine("    BACKGROUND-COLOR: black;")
txtstream.WriteLine("        FONT-FAMILY: font-family:  Cambria, serif;")
txtstream.WriteLine("    FONT-SIZE: 12px;")
txtstream.WriteLine("    text-align: left;")
txtstream.WriteLine("    white-Space: nowrap;")
txtstream.WriteLine(" Next")
txtstream.WriteLine("div")
txtstream.WriteLine("")
```

```
txtstream.WriteLine("    COLOR: white;")
txtstream.WriteLine("    BACKGROUND-COLOR: black;")
txtstream.WriteLine("        FONT-FAMILY: font-family: Cambria,
serif;")
txtstream.WriteLine("    FONT-SIZE: 10px;")
txtstream.WriteLine("    text-align: left;")
txtstream.WriteLine("    white-Space: nowrap;")
txtstream.WriteLine(" Next")
txtstream.WriteLine("span")
txtstream.WriteLine("")
txtstream.WriteLine("    COLOR: white;")
txtstream.WriteLine("    BACKGROUND-COLOR: black;")
txtstream.WriteLine("        FONT-FAMILY: font-family: Cambria,
serif;")
txtstream.WriteLine("    FONT-SIZE: 10px;")
txtstream.WriteLine("    text-align: left;")
txtstream.WriteLine("    white-Space: nowrap;")
txtstream.WriteLine("    display:inline-block;")
txtstream.WriteLine("    width: 100%;")
txtstream.WriteLine(" Next")
txtstream.WriteLine("textarea")
txtstream.WriteLine("")
txtstream.WriteLine("    COLOR: white;")
txtstream.WriteLine("    BACKGROUND-COLOR: black;")
```

txtstream.WriteLine("   FONT-FAMILY: font-family: Cambria, serif;")

txtstream.WriteLine("   FONT-SIZE: 10px;")

txtstream.WriteLine("   text-align: left;")

txtstream.WriteLine("   white-Space: nowrap;")

txtstream.WriteLine("   width: 100%;")

txtstream.WriteLine(" Next")

txtstream.WriteLine("select")

txtstream.WriteLine("'")

txtstream.WriteLine("   COLOR: white;")

txtstream.WriteLine("   BACKGROUND-COLOR: black;")

txtstream.WriteLine("   FONT-FAMILY: font-family: Cambria, serif;")

txtstream.WriteLine("   FONT-SIZE: 10px;")

txtstream.WriteLine("   text-align: left;")

txtstream.WriteLine("   white-Space: nowrap;")

txtstream.WriteLine("   width: 100%;")

txtstream.WriteLine(" Next")

txtstream.WriteLine("input")

txtstream.WriteLine("'")

txtstream.WriteLine("   COLOR: white;")

txtstream.WriteLine("   BACKGROUND-COLOR: black;")

txtstream.WriteLine("   FONT-FAMILY: font-family: Cambria, serif;")

txtstream.WriteLine("   FONT-SIZE: 12px;")

txtstream.WriteLine("   text-align: left;")

txtstream.WriteLine("   display:table-cell;")

txtstream.WriteLine("   white-Space: nowrap;")

txtstream.WriteLine(" Next")

txtstream.WriteLine("h1 ")

txtstream.WriteLine("color: antiquewhite;")

txtstream.WriteLine("text-shadow: 1px 1px 1px black;")

txtstream.WriteLine("padding: 3px;")

txtstream.WriteLine("text-align: center;")

txtstream.WriteLine("box-shadow: inSet 2px 2px 5px rgba(0,0,0,0.5), inSet -2px -2px 5px rgba(255,255,255,0.5);")

txtstream.WriteLine(" Next")

txtstream.WriteLine("</style>")

COLORED TEXT

txtstream.WriteLine("<style type='text/css'>")

txtstream.WriteLine("th")

txtstream.WriteLine("")

txtstream.WriteLine("   COLOR: darkred;")

txtstream.WriteLine("   BACKGROUND-COLOR: #eeeeee;")

txtstream.WriteLine("   FONT-FAMILY:font-family: Cambria, serif;")

txtstream.WriteLine("   FONT-SIZE: 12px;")

txtstream.WriteLine("   text-align: left;")

txtstream.WriteLine("   white-Space: nowrap;")

```
txtstream.WriteLine(" Next")
txtstream.WriteLine("td")
txtstream.WriteLine("'")
txtstream.WriteLine("    COLOR: navy;")
txtstream.WriteLine("    BACKGROUND-COLOR: #eeeeee;")
txtstream.WriteLine("      FONT-FAMILY: font-family: Cambria,
serif;")
txtstream.WriteLine("    FONT-SIZE: 12px;")
txtstream.WriteLine("    text-align: left;")
txtstream.WriteLine("    white-Space: nowrap;")
txtstream.WriteLine(" Next")
txtstream.WriteLine("div")
txtstream.WriteLine("'")
txtstream.WriteLine("    COLOR: white;")
txtstream.WriteLine("    BACKGROUND-COLOR: navy;")
txtstream.WriteLine("      FONT-FAMILY: font-family: Cambria,
serif;")
txtstream.WriteLine("    FONT-SIZE: 10px;")
txtstream.WriteLine("    text-align: left;")
txtstream.WriteLine("    white-Space: nowrap;")
txtstream.WriteLine(" Next")
txtstream.WriteLine("span")
txtstream.WriteLine("'")
txtstream.WriteLine("    COLOR: white;")
txtstream.WriteLine("    BACKGROUND-COLOR: navy;")
```

txtstream.WriteLine("   FONT-FAMILY: font-family: Cambria, serif;")

txtstream.WriteLine("   FONT-SIZE: 10px;")

txtstream.WriteLine("   text-align: left;")

txtstream.WriteLine("   white-Space: nowrap;")

txtstream.WriteLine("   display:inline-block;")

txtstream.WriteLine("   width: 100%;")

txtstream.WriteLine(" Next")

txtstream.WriteLine("textarea")

txtstream.WriteLine("'")

txtstream.WriteLine("   COLOR: white;")

txtstream.WriteLine("   BACKGROUND-COLOR: navy;")

txtstream.WriteLine("   FONT-FAMILY: font-family: Cambria, serif;")

txtstream.WriteLine("   FONT-SIZE: 10px;")

txtstream.WriteLine("   text-align: left;")

txtstream.WriteLine("   white-Space: nowrap;")

txtstream.WriteLine("   width: 100%;")

txtstream.WriteLine(" Next")

txtstream.WriteLine("select")

txtstream.WriteLine("'")

txtstream.WriteLine("   COLOR: white;")

txtstream.WriteLine("   BACKGROUND-COLOR: navy;")

txtstream.WriteLine("   FONT-FAMILY: font-family: Cambria, serif;")

```
txtstream.WriteLine("    FONT-SIZE: 10px;")
txtstream.WriteLine("    text-align: left;")
txtstream.WriteLine("    white-Space: nowrap;")
txtstream.WriteLine("    width: 100%;")
txtstream.WriteLine(" Next")
txtstream.WriteLine("input")
txtstream.WriteLine("'")
txtstream.WriteLine("    COLOR: white;")
txtstream.WriteLine("    BACKGROUND-COLOR: navy;")
txtstream.WriteLine("        FONT-FAMILY: font-family: Cambria, serif;")
txtstream.WriteLine("    FONT-SIZE: 12px;")
txtstream.WriteLine("    text-align: left;")
txtstream.WriteLine("    display:table-cell;")
txtstream.WriteLine("    white-Space: nowrap;")
txtstream.WriteLine(" Next")
txtstream.WriteLine("h1 '")
txtstream.WriteLine("color: antiquewhite;")
txtstream.WriteLine("text-shadow: 1px 1px 1px black;")
txtstream.WriteLine("padding: 3px;")
txtstream.WriteLine("text-align: center;")
txtstream.WriteLine("box-shadow: inSet 2px 2px 5px rgba(0,0,0,0.5), inSet -2px -2px 5px rgba(255,255,255,0.5);")
txtstream.WriteLine(" Next")
txtstream.WriteLine("</style>'")
```

OSCILLATING ROW COLORS

txtstream.WriteLine("<style>")

txtstream.WriteLine("th")

txtstream.WriteLine("")

txtstream.WriteLine("   COLOR: white;")

txtstream.WriteLine("   BACKGROUND-COLOR: navy;")

txtstream.WriteLine("   FONT-FAMILY:font-family: Cambria, serif;")

txtstream.WriteLine("   FONT-SIZE: 12px;")

txtstream.WriteLine("   text-align: left;")

txtstream.WriteLine("   white-Space: nowrap;")

txtstream.WriteLine(" Next")

txtstream.WriteLine("td")

txtstream.WriteLine("")

txtstream.WriteLine("   COLOR: navy;")

txtstream.WriteLine("   FONT-FAMILY: font-family: Cambria, serif;")

txtstream.WriteLine("   FONT-SIZE: 12px;")

txtstream.WriteLine("   text-align: left;")

txtstream.WriteLine("   white-Space: nowrap;")

txtstream.WriteLine(" Next")

```
txtstream.WriteLine("div")

txtstream.WriteLine("'

txtstream.WriteLine("    COLOR: navy;")

txtstream.WriteLine("        FONT-FAMILY: font-family: Cambria,
serif;")

txtstream.WriteLine("    FONT-SIZE: 12px;")

txtstream.WriteLine("    text-align: left;")

txtstream.WriteLine("    white-Space: nowrap;")

txtstream.WriteLine(" Next")

txtstream.WriteLine("span")

txtstream.WriteLine("'

txtstream.WriteLine("    COLOR: navy;")

txtstream.WriteLine("        FONT-FAMILY: font-family: Cambria,
serif;")

txtstream.WriteLine("    FONT-SIZE: 12px;")

txtstream.WriteLine("    text-align: left;")

txtstream.WriteLine("    white-Space: nowrap;")

txtstream.WriteLine("    width: 100%;")

txtstream.WriteLine(" Next")

txtstream.WriteLine("textarea")

txtstream.WriteLine("'

txtstream.WriteLine("    COLOR: navy;")

txtstream.WriteLine("        FONT-FAMILY: font-family: Cambria,
serif;")

txtstream.WriteLine("    FONT-SIZE: 12px;")
```

```
txtstream.WriteLine("    text-align: left;")
txtstream.WriteLine("    white-Space: nowrap;")
txtstream.WriteLine("    display:inline-block;")
txtstream.WriteLine("    width: 100%;")
txtstream.WriteLine(" Next")
txtstream.WriteLine("select")
txtstream.WriteLine("")
txtstream.WriteLine("    COLOR: navy;")
txtstream.WriteLine("        FONT-FAMILY: font-family: Cambria, serif;")
txtstream.WriteLine("    FONT-SIZE: 10px;")
txtstream.WriteLine("    text-align: left;")
txtstream.WriteLine("    white-Space: nowrap;")
txtstream.WriteLine("    display:inline-block;")
txtstream.WriteLine("    width: 100%;")
txtstream.WriteLine(" Next")
txtstream.WriteLine("input")
txtstream.WriteLine("")
txtstream.WriteLine("    COLOR: navy;")
txtstream.WriteLine("        FONT-FAMILY: font-family: Cambria, serif;")
txtstream.WriteLine("    FONT-SIZE: 12px;")
txtstream.WriteLine("    text-align: left;")
txtstream.WriteLine("    display:table-cell;")
txtstream.WriteLine("    white-Space: nowrap;")
```

txtstream.WriteLine(" Next")

txtstream.WriteLine("h1 ")

txtstream.WriteLine("color: antiquewhite;")

txtstream.WriteLine("text-shadow: 1px 1px 1px black;")

txtstream.WriteLine("padding: 3px;")

txtstream.WriteLine("text-align: center;")

txtstream.WriteLine("box-shadow: inSet 2px 2px 5px rgba(0,0,0,0.5), inSet -2px -2px 5px rgba(255,255,255,0.5);")

txtstream.WriteLine(" Next")

txtstream.WriteLine("tr:nth-child(even)background-color:#f2f2f2; Next")

txtstream.WriteLine("tr:nth-child(odd)background-color:#cccccc; color:#f2f2f2; Next")

txtstream.WriteLine("</style>")

GHOST DECORATED

txtstream.WriteLine("<style type='text/css'>")

txtstream.WriteLine("th")

txtstream.WriteLine("")

txtstream.WriteLine("   COLOR: black;")

txtstream.WriteLine("   BACKGROUND-COLOR: white;")

txtstream.WriteLine("   FONT-FAMILY:font-family: Cambria, serif;")

txtstream.WriteLine("   FONT-SIZE: 12px;")

txtstream.WriteLine("   text-align: left;")

txtstream.WriteLine("   white-Space: nowrap;")

txtstream.WriteLine(" Next")

txtstream.WriteLine("td")

txtstream.WriteLine("'")

txtstream.WriteLine("   COLOR: black;")

txtstream.WriteLine("   BACKGROUND-COLOR: white;")

txtstream.WriteLine("   FONT-FAMILY: font-family: Cambria, serif;")

txtstream.WriteLine("   FONT-SIZE: 12px;")

txtstream.WriteLine("   text-align: left;")

txtstream.WriteLine("   white-Space: nowrap;")

txtstream.WriteLine(" Next")

txtstream.WriteLine("div")

txtstream.WriteLine("'")

txtstream.WriteLine("   COLOR: black;")

txtstream.WriteLine("   BACKGROUND-COLOR: white;")

txtstream.WriteLine("   FONT-FAMILY: font-family: Cambria, serif;")

txtstream.WriteLine("   FONT-SIZE: 10px;")

txtstream.WriteLine("   text-align: left;")

txtstream.WriteLine("   white-Space: nowrap;")

txtstream.WriteLine(" Next")

txtstream.WriteLine("span")

txtstream.WriteLine("'")

```
txtstream.WriteLine("    COLOR: black;")
txtstream.WriteLine("    BACKGROUND-COLOR: white;")
txtstream.WriteLine("        FONT-FAMILY: font-family: Cambria,
serif;")
txtstream.WriteLine("    FONT-SIZE: 10px;")
txtstream.WriteLine("    text-align: left;")
txtstream.WriteLine("    white-Space: nowrap;")
txtstream.WriteLine("    display:inline-block;")
txtstream.WriteLine("    width: 100%;")
txtstream.WriteLine(" Next")
txtstream.WriteLine("textarea")
txtstream.WriteLine(""")
txtstream.WriteLine("    COLOR: black;")
txtstream.WriteLine("    BACKGROUND-COLOR: white;")
txtstream.WriteLine("        FONT-FAMILY: font-family: Cambria,
serif;")
txtstream.WriteLine("    FONT-SIZE: 10px;")
txtstream.WriteLine("    text-align: left;")
txtstream.WriteLine("    white-Space: nowrap;")
txtstream.WriteLine("    width: 100%;")
txtstream.WriteLine(" Next")
txtstream.WriteLine("select")
txtstream.WriteLine(""")
txtstream.WriteLine("    COLOR: black;")
txtstream.WriteLine("    BACKGROUND-COLOR: white;")
```

txtstream.WriteLine("   FONT-FAMILY: font-family: Cambria, serif;")

txtstream.WriteLine("   FONT-SIZE: 10px;")

txtstream.WriteLine("   text-align: left;")

txtstream.WriteLine("   white-Space: nowrap;")

txtstream.WriteLine("   width: 100%;")

txtstream.WriteLine(" Next")

txtstream.WriteLine("input")

txtstream.WriteLine("")

txtstream.WriteLine("   COLOR: black;")

txtstream.WriteLine("   BACKGROUND-COLOR: white;")

txtstream.WriteLine("   FONT-FAMILY: font-family: Cambria, serif;")

txtstream.WriteLine("   FONT-SIZE: 12px;")

txtstream.WriteLine("   text-align: left;")

txtstream.WriteLine("   display:table-cell;")

txtstream.WriteLine("   white-Space: nowrap;")

txtstream.WriteLine(" Next")

txtstream.WriteLine("h1 ")

txtstream.WriteLine("color: antiquewhite;")

txtstream.WriteLine("text-shadow: 1px 1px 1px black;")

txtstream.WriteLine("padding: 3px;")

txtstream.WriteLine("text-align: center;")

txtstream.WriteLine("box-shadow: inSet 2px 2px 5px rgba(0,0,0,0.5), inSet -2px -2px 5px rgba(255,255,255,0.5);")

txtstream.WriteLine(" Next")

txtstream.WriteLine("</style>")

3D

txtstream.WriteLine("<style type='text/css'>")

txtstream.WriteLine("body")

txtstream.WriteLine("")

txtstream.WriteLine("   PADDING-RIGHT: 0px;")

txtstream.WriteLine("   PADDING-LEFT: 0px;")

txtstream.WriteLine("   PADDING-BOTTOM: 0px;")

txtstream.WriteLine("   MARGIN: 0px;")

txtstream.WriteLine("   COLOR: #333;")

txtstream.WriteLine("   PADDING-TOP: 0px;")

txtstream.WriteLine("   FONT-FAMILY: verdana, arial, helvetica, sans-serif;")

txtstream.WriteLine(" Next")

txtstream.WriteLine("table")

txtstream.WriteLine("")

txtstream.WriteLine("   BORDER-RIGHT: #999999 3px solid;")

txtstream.WriteLine("   PADDING-RIGHT: 6px;")

txtstream.WriteLine("   PADDING-LEFT: 6px;")

txtstream.WriteLine("   FONT-WEIGHT: Bold;")

txtstream.WriteLine("   FONT-SIZE: 14px;")

```
txtstream.WriteLine("    PADDING-BOTTOM: 6px;")
txtstream.WriteLine("    COLOR: Peru;")
txtstream.WriteLine("    LINE-HEIGHT: 14px;")
txtstream.WriteLine("    PADDING-TOP: 6px;")
txtstream.WriteLine("    BORDER-BOTTOM: #999 1px solid;")
txtstream.WriteLine("    BACKGROUND-COLOR: #eeeeee;")
txtstream.WriteLine("    FONT-FAMILY: verdana, arial, helvetica, sans-serif;")
txtstream.WriteLine("    FONT-SIZE: 12px;")
txtstream.WriteLine(" Next")
txtstream.WriteLine("th")
txtstream.WriteLine("'")
txtstream.WriteLine("    BORDER-RIGHT: #999999 3px solid;")
txtstream.WriteLine("    PADDING-RIGHT: 6px;")
txtstream.WriteLine("    PADDING-LEFT: 6px;")
txtstream.WriteLine("    FONT-WEIGHT: Bold;")
txtstream.WriteLine("    FONT-SIZE: 14px;")
txtstream.WriteLine("    PADDING-BOTTOM: 6px;")
txtstream.WriteLine("    COLOR: darkred;")
txtstream.WriteLine("    LINE-HEIGHT: 14px;")
txtstream.WriteLine("    PADDING-TOP: 6px;")
txtstream.WriteLine("    BORDER-BOTTOM: #999 1px solid;")
txtstream.WriteLine("    BACKGROUND-COLOR: #eeeeee;")
txtstream.WriteLine("    FONT-FAMILY:font-family: Cambria, serif;")
```

```
txtstream.WriteLine("    FONT-SIZE: 12px;")
txtstream.WriteLine("    text-align: left;")
txtstream.WriteLine("    white-Space: nowrap;")
txtstream.WriteLine(" Next")
txtstream.WriteLine(".th")
txtstream.WriteLine("'")
txtstream.WriteLine("    BORDER-RIGHT: #999999 2px solid;")
txtstream.WriteLine("    PADDING-RIGHT: 6px;")
txtstream.WriteLine("    PADDING-LEFT: 6px;")
txtstream.WriteLine("    FONT-WEIGHT: Bold;")
txtstream.WriteLine("    PADDING-BOTTOM: 6px;")
txtstream.WriteLine("    COLOR: black;")
txtstream.WriteLine("    PADDING-TOP: 6px;")
txtstream.WriteLine("    BORDER-BOTTOM: #999 2px solid;")
txtstream.WriteLine("    BACKGROUND-COLOR: #eeeeee;")
txtstream.WriteLine("       FONT-FAMILY:  font-family:  Cambria,
serif;")
txtstream.WriteLine("    FONT-SIZE: 10px;")
txtstream.WriteLine("    text-align: right;")
txtstream.WriteLine("    white-Space: nowrap;")
txtstream.WriteLine(" Next")
txtstream.WriteLine("td")
txtstream.WriteLine("'")
txtstream.WriteLine("    BORDER-RIGHT: #999999 3px solid;")
txtstream.WriteLine("    PADDING-RIGHT: 6px;")
```

```
txtstream.WriteLine("    PADDING-LEFT: 6px;")
txtstream.WriteLine("    FONT-WEIGHT: Normal;")
txtstream.WriteLine("    PADDING-BOTTOM: 6px;")
txtstream.WriteLine("    COLOR: navy;")
txtstream.WriteLine("    LINE-HEIGHT: 14px;")
txtstream.WriteLine("    PADDING-TOP: 6px;")
txtstream.WriteLine("    BORDER-BOTTOM: #999 1px solid;")
txtstream.WriteLine("    BACKGROUND-COLOR: #eeeeee;")
txtstream.WriteLine("        FONT-FAMILY:  font-family:  Cambria,
serif;")
txtstream.WriteLine("    FONT-SIZE: 12px;")
txtstream.WriteLine("    text-align: left;")
txtstream.WriteLine("    white-Space: nowrap;")
txtstream.WriteLine(" Next")
txtstream.WriteLine("div")
txtstream.WriteLine("'")
txtstream.WriteLine("    BORDER-RIGHT: #999999 3px solid;")
txtstream.WriteLine("    PADDING-RIGHT: 6px;")
txtstream.WriteLine("    PADDING-LEFT: 6px;")
txtstream.WriteLine("    FONT-WEIGHT: Normal;")
txtstream.WriteLine("    PADDING-BOTTOM: 6px;")
txtstream.WriteLine("    COLOR: white;")
txtstream.WriteLine("    PADDING-TOP: 6px;")
txtstream.WriteLine("    BORDER-BOTTOM: #999 1px solid;")
txtstream.WriteLine("    BACKGROUND-COLOR: navy;")
```

txtstream.WriteLine("   FONT-FAMILY: font-family: Cambria, serif;")

txtstream.WriteLine("   FONT-SIZE: 10px;")

txtstream.WriteLine("   text-align: left;")

txtstream.WriteLine("   white-Space: nowrap;")

txtstream.WriteLine(" Next")

txtstream.WriteLine("span")

txtstream.WriteLine(""")

txtstream.WriteLine("   BORDER-RIGHT: #999999 3px solid;")

txtstream.WriteLine("   PADDING-RIGHT: 3px;")

txtstream.WriteLine("   PADDING-LEFT: 3px;")

txtstream.WriteLine("   FONT-WEIGHT: Normal;")

txtstream.WriteLine("   PADDING-BOTTOM: 3px;")

txtstream.WriteLine("   COLOR: white;")

txtstream.WriteLine("   PADDING-TOP: 3px;")

txtstream.WriteLine("   BORDER-BOTTOM: #999 1px solid;")

txtstream.WriteLine("   BACKGROUND-COLOR: navy;")

txtstream.WriteLine("   FONT-FAMILY: font-family: Cambria, serif;")

txtstream.WriteLine("   FONT-SIZE: 10px;")

txtstream.WriteLine("   text-align: left;")

txtstream.WriteLine("   white-Space: nowrap;")

txtstream.WriteLine("   display:inline-block;")

txtstream.WriteLine("   width: 100%;")

txtstream.WriteLine(" Next")

```
txtstream.WriteLine("textarea")
txtstream.WriteLine("{")
txtstream.WriteLine("    BORDER-RIGHT: #999999 3px solid;")
txtstream.WriteLine("    PADDING-RIGHT: 3px;")
txtstream.WriteLine("    PADDING-LEFT: 3px;")
txtstream.WriteLine("    FONT-WEIGHT: Normal;")
txtstream.WriteLine("    PADDING-BOTTOM: 3px;")
txtstream.WriteLine("    COLOR: white;")
txtstream.WriteLine("    PADDING-TOP: 3px;")
txtstream.WriteLine("    BORDER-BOTTOM: #999 1px solid;")
txtstream.WriteLine("    BACKGROUND-COLOR: navy;")
txtstream.WriteLine("        FONT-FAMILY: font-family: Cambria, serif;")
txtstream.WriteLine("    FONT-SIZE: 10px;")
txtstream.WriteLine("    text-align: left;")
txtstream.WriteLine("    white-Space: nowrap;")
txtstream.WriteLine("    width: 100%;")
txtstream.WriteLine(" Next")
txtstream.WriteLine("select")
txtstream.WriteLine("{")
txtstream.WriteLine("    BORDER-RIGHT: #999999 3px solid;")
txtstream.WriteLine("    PADDING-RIGHT: 6px;")
txtstream.WriteLine("    PADDING-LEFT: 6px;")
txtstream.WriteLine("    FONT-WEIGHT: Normal;")
txtstream.WriteLine("    PADDING-BOTTOM: 6px;")
```

```
txtstream.WriteLine("    COLOR: white;")
txtstream.WriteLine("    PADDING-TOP: 6px;")
txtstream.WriteLine("    BORDER-BOTTOM: #999 1px solid;")
txtstream.WriteLine("    BACKGROUND-COLOR: navy;")
txtstream.WriteLine("    FONT-FAMILY: font-family: Cambria, serif;")
txtstream.WriteLine("    FONT-SIZE: 10px;")
txtstream.WriteLine("    text-align: left;")
txtstream.WriteLine("    white-Space: nowrap;")
txtstream.WriteLine("    width: 100%;")
txtstream.WriteLine(" Next")
txtstream.WriteLine("input")
txtstream.WriteLine("'")
txtstream.WriteLine("    BORDER-RIGHT: #999999 3px solid;")
txtstream.WriteLine("    PADDING-RIGHT: 3px;")
txtstream.WriteLine("    PADDING-LEFT: 3px;")
txtstream.WriteLine("    FONT-WEIGHT: Bold;")
txtstream.WriteLine("    PADDING-BOTTOM: 3px;")
txtstream.WriteLine("    COLOR: white;")
txtstream.WriteLine("    PADDING-TOP: 3px;")
txtstream.WriteLine("    BORDER-BOTTOM: #999 1px solid;")
txtstream.WriteLine("    BACKGROUND-COLOR: navy;")
txtstream.WriteLine("    FONT-FAMILY: font-family: Cambria, serif;")
txtstream.WriteLine("    FONT-SIZE: 12px;")
```

txtstream.WriteLine("   text-align: left;")

txtstream.WriteLine("   display:table-cell;")

txtstream.WriteLine("   white-Space: nowrap;")

txtstream.WriteLine("   width: 100%;")

txtstream.WriteLine(" Next")

txtstream.WriteLine("h1 ")

txtstream.WriteLine("color: antiquewhite;")

txtstream.WriteLine("text-shadow: 1px 1px 1px black;")

txtstream.WriteLine("padding: 3px;")

txtstream.WriteLine("text-align: center;")

txtstream.WriteLine("box-shadow: inSet 2px 2px 5px rgba(0,0,0,0.5), inSet -2px -2px 5px rgba(255,255,255,0.5);")

txtstream.WriteLine(" Next")

txtstream.WriteLine("</style>")

SHADOW BOX

txtstream.WriteLine("<style type='text/css'>")

txtstream.WriteLine("body")

txtstream.WriteLine("")

txtstream.WriteLine("   PADDING-RIGHT: 0px;")

txtstream.WriteLine("   PADDING-LEFT: 0px;")

txtstream.WriteLine("   PADDING-BOTTOM: 0px;")

txtstream.WriteLine("   MARGIN: 0px;")

txtstream.WriteLine("   COLOR: #333;")

```
txtstream.WriteLine("    PADDING-TOP: 0px;")
txtstream.WriteLine("      FONT-FAMILY: verdana, arial, helvetica,
sans-serif;")
txtstream.WriteLine(" Next")
txtstream.WriteLine("table")
txtstream.WriteLine(""
txtstream.WriteLine("    BORDER-RIGHT: #999999 1px solid;")
txtstream.WriteLine("    PADDING-RIGHT: 1px;")
txtstream.WriteLine("    PADDING-LEFT: 1px;")
txtstream.WriteLine("    PADDING-BOTTOM: 1px;")
txtstream.WriteLine("    LINE-HEIGHT: 8px;")
txtstream.WriteLine("    PADDING-TOP: 1px;")
txtstream.WriteLine("    BORDER-BOTTOM: #999 1px solid;")
txtstream.WriteLine("    BACKGROUND-COLOR: #eeeeee;")
txtstream.WriteLine("
filter:progid:DXImageTransform.Microsoft.Shadow(color='silver',
Direction=135, Strength=16)")
txtstream.WriteLine(" Next")
txtstream.WriteLine("th")
txtstream.WriteLine(""
txtstream.WriteLine("    BORDER-RIGHT: #999999 3px solid;")
txtstream.WriteLine("    PADDING-RIGHT: 6px;")
txtstream.WriteLine("    PADDING-LEFT: 6px;")
txtstream.WriteLine("    FONT-WEIGHT: Bold;")
txtstream.WriteLine("    FONT-SIZE: 14px;")
```

txtstream.WriteLine("   PADDING-BOTTOM: 6px;")

txtstream.WriteLine("   COLOR: darkred;")

txtstream.WriteLine("   LINE-HEIGHT: 14px;")

txtstream.WriteLine("   PADDING-TOP: 6px;")

txtstream.WriteLine("   BORDER-BOTTOM: #999 1px solid;")

txtstream.WriteLine("   BACKGROUND-COLOR: #eeeeee;")

txtstream.WriteLine("   FONT-FAMILY: font-family: Cambria,
serif;")

txtstream.WriteLine("   FONT-SIZE: 12px;")

txtstream.WriteLine("   text-align: left;")

txtstream.WriteLine("   white-Space: nowrap;")

txtstream.WriteLine(" Next")

txtstream.WriteLine(".th")

txtstream.WriteLine("")

txtstream.WriteLine("   BORDER-RIGHT: #999999 2px solid;")

txtstream.WriteLine("   PADDING-RIGHT: 6px;")

txtstream.WriteLine("   PADDING-LEFT: 6px;")

txtstream.WriteLine("   FONT-WEIGHT: Bold;")

txtstream.WriteLine("   PADDING-BOTTOM: 6px;")

txtstream.WriteLine("   COLOR: black;")

txtstream.WriteLine("   PADDING-TOP: 6px;")

txtstream.WriteLine("   BORDER-BOTTOM: #999 2px solid;")

txtstream.WriteLine("   BACKGROUND-COLOR: #eeeeee;")

txtstream.WriteLine("   FONT-FAMILY: font-family: Cambria,
serif;")

```
txtstream.WriteLine("    FONT-SIZE: 10px;")
txtstream.WriteLine("    text-align: right;")
txtstream.WriteLine("    white-Space: nowrap;")
txtstream.WriteLine(" Next")
txtstream.WriteLine("td")
txtstream.WriteLine("")
txtstream.WriteLine("    BORDER-RIGHT: #999999 3px solid;")
txtstream.WriteLine("    PADDING-RIGHT: 6px;")
txtstream.WriteLine("    PADDING-LEFT: 6px;")
txtstream.WriteLine("    FONT-WEIGHT: Normal;")
txtstream.WriteLine("    PADDING-BOTTOM: 6px;")
txtstream.WriteLine("    COLOR: navy;")
txtstream.WriteLine("    LINE-HEIGHT: 14px;")
txtstream.WriteLine("    PADDING-TOP: 6px;")
txtstream.WriteLine("    BORDER-BOTTOM: #999 1px solid;")
txtstream.WriteLine("    BACKGROUND-COLOR: #eeeeee;")
txtstream.WriteLine("        FONT-FAMILY:  font-family:  Cambria,
serif;")
txtstream.WriteLine("    FONT-SIZE: 12px;")
txtstream.WriteLine("    text-align: left;")
txtstream.WriteLine("    white-Space: nowrap;")
txtstream.WriteLine(" Next")
txtstream.WriteLine("div")
txtstream.WriteLine("")
txtstream.WriteLine("    BORDER-RIGHT: #999999 3px solid;")
```

```
txtstream.WriteLine("    PADDING-RIGHT: 6px;")
txtstream.WriteLine("    PADDING-LEFT: 6px;")
txtstream.WriteLine("    FONT-WEIGHT: Normal;")
txtstream.WriteLine("    PADDING-BOTTOM: 6px;")
txtstream.WriteLine("    COLOR: white;")
txtstream.WriteLine("    PADDING-TOP: 6px;")
txtstream.WriteLine("    BORDER-BOTTOM: #999 1px solid;")
txtstream.WriteLine("    BACKGROUND-COLOR: navy;")
txtstream.WriteLine("        FONT-FAMILY: font-family: Cambria,
serif;")
txtstream.WriteLine("    FONT-SIZE: 10px;")
txtstream.WriteLine("    text-align: left;")
txtstream.WriteLine("    white-Space: nowrap;")
txtstream.WriteLine(" Next")
txtstream.WriteLine("span")
txtstream.WriteLine("")
txtstream.WriteLine("    BORDER-RIGHT: #999999 3px solid;")
txtstream.WriteLine("    PADDING-RIGHT: 3px;")
txtstream.WriteLine("    PADDING-LEFT: 3px;")
txtstream.WriteLine("    FONT-WEIGHT: Normal;")
txtstream.WriteLine("    PADDING-BOTTOM: 3px;")
txtstream.WriteLine("    COLOR: white;")
txtstream.WriteLine("    PADDING-TOP: 3px;")
txtstream.WriteLine("    BORDER-BOTTOM: #999 1px solid;")
txtstream.WriteLine("    BACKGROUND-COLOR: navy;")
```

txtstream.WriteLine("   FONT-FAMILY: font-family: Cambria, serif;")

txtstream.WriteLine("   FONT-SIZE: 10px;")

txtstream.WriteLine("   text-align: left;")

txtstream.WriteLine("   white-Space: nowrap;")

txtstream.WriteLine("   display: inline-block;")

txtstream.WriteLine("   width: 100%;")

txtstream.WriteLine(" Next")

txtstream.WriteLine("textarea")

txtstream.WriteLine("")

txtstream.WriteLine("   BORDER-RIGHT: #999999 3px solid;")

txtstream.WriteLine("   PADDING-RIGHT: 3px;")

txtstream.WriteLine("   PADDING-LEFT: 3px;")

txtstream.WriteLine("   FONT-WEIGHT: Normal;")

txtstream.WriteLine("   PADDING-BOTTOM: 3px;")

txtstream.WriteLine("   COLOR: white;")

txtstream.WriteLine("   PADDING-TOP: 3px;")

txtstream.WriteLine("   BORDER-BOTTOM: #999 1px solid;")

txtstream.WriteLine("   BACKGROUND-COLOR: navy;")

txtstream.WriteLine("   FONT-FAMILY: font-family: Cambria, serif;")

txtstream.WriteLine("   FONT-SIZE: 10px;")

txtstream.WriteLine("   text-align: left;")

txtstream.WriteLine("   white-Space: nowrap;")

txtstream.WriteLine("   width: 100%;")

txtstream.WriteLine(" Next")

txtstream.WriteLine("select")

txtstream.WriteLine("'")

txtstream.WriteLine("   BORDER-RIGHT: #999999 3px solid;")

txtstream.WriteLine("   PADDING-RIGHT: 6px;")

txtstream.WriteLine("   PADDING-LEFT: 6px;")

txtstream.WriteLine("   FONT-WEIGHT: Normal;")

txtstream.WriteLine("   PADDING-BOTTOM: 6px;")

txtstream.WriteLine("   COLOR: white;")

txtstream.WriteLine("   PADDING-TOP: 6px;")

txtstream.WriteLine("   BORDER-BOTTOM: #999 1px solid;")

txtstream.WriteLine("   BACKGROUND-COLOR: navy;")

txtstream.WriteLine("   FONT-FAMILY: font-family: Cambria, serif;")

txtstream.WriteLine("   FONT-SIZE: 10px;")

txtstream.WriteLine("   text-align: left;")

txtstream.WriteLine("   white-Space: nowrap;")

txtstream.WriteLine("   width: 100%;")

txtstream.WriteLine(" Next")

txtstream.WriteLine("input")

txtstream.WriteLine("'")

txtstream.WriteLine("   BORDER-RIGHT: #999999 3px solid;")

txtstream.WriteLine("   PADDING-RIGHT: 3px;")

txtstream.WriteLine("   PADDING-LEFT: 3px;")

txtstream.WriteLine("   FONT-WEIGHT: Bold;")

```
txtstream.WriteLine("    PADDING-BOTTOM: 3px;")
txtstream.WriteLine("    COLOR: white;")
txtstream.WriteLine("    PADDING-TOP: 3px;")
txtstream.WriteLine("    BORDER-BOTTOM: #999 1px solid;")
txtstream.WriteLine("    BACKGROUND-COLOR: navy;")
txtstream.WriteLine("      FONT-FAMILY:  font-family:  Cambria, serif;")
txtstream.WriteLine("    FONT-SIZE: 12px;")
txtstream.WriteLine("    text-align: left;")
txtstream.WriteLine("    display: table-cell;")
txtstream.WriteLine("    white-Space: nowrap;")
txtstream.WriteLine("    width: 100%;")
txtstream.WriteLine(" Next")
txtstream.WriteLine("h1 ")
txtstream.WriteLine("color: antiquewhite;")
txtstream.WriteLine("text-shadow: 1px 1px 1px black;")
txtstream.WriteLine("padding: 3px;")
txtstream.WriteLine("text-align: center;")
txtstream.WriteLine("box-shadow: inSet 2px 2px 5px rgba(0,0,0,0.5), inSet -2px -2px 5px rgba(255,255,255,0.5);")
txtstream.WriteLine(" Next")
txtstream.WriteLine("</style>")
```

www.ingramcontent.com/pod-product-compliance
Lightning Source LLC
Chambersburg PA
CBHW071141050326
40690CB00008B/1533